A Book of Reformed Prayers

ALSO FROM
WESTMINSTER JOHN KNOX PRESS

By Howard L. Rice
Reformed Spirituality: An Introduction for Believers

By Lamar Williamson, Jr.
Mark (Interpretation series)

A Book of Reformed Prayers

Howard L. Rice
Lamar Williamson, Jr.
editors

Westminster John Knox Press
Louisville, Kentucky

Book and cover design by Jennifer K. Cox
Art © 1998 PhotoDisc, Inc.

First edition
Published by Westminster John Knox Press
Louisville, Kentucky

This book is printed on acid-free paper that meets the
American National Standards Institute Z39.48 standard. ♾

PRINTED IN THE UNITED STATES OF AMERICA
98 99 00 01 02 03 04 05 06 07 — 10 9 8 7 6 5 4 3 2 1

Library of Congress Cataloging-in-Publication Data

A book of Reformed prayers / Howard L. Rice, Lamar Williamson, Jr.,
   editors
        p.   cm.
   ISBN 0-664-25701-1
   1. Reformed Church—Prayer-books and devotions—English.
2. Prayer—Reformed Church.   3. Prayers.   I. Rice, Howard L.
II. Williamson, Lamar.
BX9427.5.P7B66 1998
242'.8042—DC21   97-28818

Contents

Acknowledgments

We wish to thank all those whose contributions to this book have been essential.

Edward Dowey of Princeton Theological Seminary found the prayers by Heinrich Bullinger for us. Cornelia Cyss-Wittenstein, a student at San Francisco Theological Seminary, translated them from the German. William O. Harris, Librarian for Archives and Special Collections at Princeton Theological Seminary, and his assistant, Raymond D. Cannata, provided and edited the prayers by Charles Hodge, Benjamin B. Warfield, and John A. Mackay. Harry Boonstra, librarian at Calvin College and Calvin Theological Seminary, secured several of the Dutch prayers. Stanley W. Bamberg of Montreat College and James E. Davison of Westminster Presbyterian Church in Pittsburgh translated them. One Dutch prayer was translated by Glen G. Baaten, a student at San Francisco Theological Seminary. Martin Prudký of Charles University in Prague secured and translated most of the prayers from Czech sources and provided information for biographical notes. Stephen Szabo, editor of the Calvin Synod Herald, United Church of Christ, secured and translated all the prayers from Hungary, assisted by Josef Posta and Helen Soos. Gérard Delteil of Montpellier, France, obtained elusive biographical data for authors of recent French prayers. Eun Chun Park, Assistant Professor of New Testament at San Francisco Theological Seminary, provided the translation of the Korean prayer by Ki-Chul Joo. Daniel Beteta, Jr., translated the prayer of his father. David Ng, who was Professor of Christian Education at San Francisco Theological Seminary, made the contact for the prayer by Greer Anne Wenh-In Ng. Warren Lee, Professor of Ministry in the Asian American Context at San Francisco Theological Seminary, translated two prayers from Korean. Hunter Farrell of the World-wide Ministries Division of the Presbyterian Church (U.S.A.) and Mary B. Crawford, retired Presbyterian missionary to Zaire, helped to locate prayers from Africa and translated two prayers from the Kasai. H. McKennie Goodpasture and Mary Jane Winter of Union Theological Seminary in Virginia helped to locate prayers from Latin America. Mark Thomas, librarian at Cook College and Theological School, helped to locate Native American prayers. Barbara and Graham Walker of First Presbyterian Church in Mesa, Arizona, secured the prayer by Dora Jackson, a Pima Indian. Marietta Yarnell of Decatur, Georgia, provided the prayer by Lawrence W. Bottoms, which she had transcribed from an audiotape. Aubrey N. Brown, Jr., of Richmond, Virginia, provided the reference for the text of the "Serenity Prayer" usually attributed to Reinhold Niebuhr. Estelle McCarthy of Richmond, Virginia, found and made available the "Prayer of Confession" by Rachel Henderlite.

Michael Peterson, branch librarian, and Alan Schreiber, assistant librarian, at San Francisco Theological Seminary provided needed help in locating sources and went beyond the call of duty to engage in searches outside the Graduate Theological Union library. Robert Benedetto, associate librarian, and Patsy Verrault, research librarian, at Union Theological Seminary in Virginia were constant sources of help, as were Elizabeth Pearson, librarian, and Julianna Bamberg, circulation assistant, at Montreat College.

We also wish to thank those who provided personal prayers—of their own or of those close to them—most of which have never before been published.

Our wives, Nancy Rice and Ruthmary Williamson, have been patient companions in this effort and have performed a valuable service in reading, editing, and critiquing the manuscript.

Introduction
How Reformed Christians Pray

Q. 98. What is prayer?

A. Prayer is an offering up of our desires unto God, for things agreeable to his will, in the name of Christ, with confession of our sins, and thankful acknowledgment of his mercies.[1]

Reformed Christians pray. One's immediate response to this statement might be a defensive, "Of course Reformed Christians pray." Such a response, while natural and correct, suggests that there are other, more obvious things that might be said about those Protestants who trace their theological heritage to the Swiss Reformation of Zwingli, Calvin, Bullinger, and their colleagues. For example, it could easily be agreed by scholars that Reformed Christians think, for careful thought has been a hallmark of this tradition, noted for its theologians such as John Calvin, Jonathan Edwards, Friedrich Schleiermacher, Charles Hodge, Karl Barth, Abraham Kuyper, Reinhold and H. Richard Niebuhr, and Jane Dempsey Douglass. Reformed Christians are noted exegetes of scripture and the tradition has produced more than its share of biblical scholars as varied as Charles A. Briggs, James Moffatt, J. Gresham Machen, John Bright, Bruce Metzger, Paul Achtemeier, Katherine Sakenfeld, and Elsa Tamez. Preaching has been a strength of Reformed Christians, and their preachers have frequently made headlines: Cotton Mather, Francis Grimké, Charles Finney, Norman Vincent Peale, Peter Marshall, and James H. Robinson. Reformed

Christians, particularly in the nineteenth and twentieth centuries, have made significant contributions to the worldwide Christian mission, to which the broad geographical scope of the prayers in this collection bears eloquent witness. One might remember, for example, David Livingston, J. Leighton Wilson, Sheldon Jackson, Donaldina Cameron, John Mackay, Darby Fulton, and Robert E. Speer. These representative figures indicate something of the power of the missionary movement among Reformed Christians. Some Reformed Christians who have distinguished themselves as political and military leaders are Jeanne d'Albret (Queen of Navarre), Oliver Cromwell, William of Orange, Andrew Jackson, Woodrow Wilson, and Dwight D. Eisenhower. In less dramatic but equally painful ways, Reformed Christians have fought one another in battles over theology and polity; the conflict over Arminianism is just one such example. And the ranks of outstanding Reformed Christians have included women, from the time of the Reformation through the current heightened concern for the role of women in the church. In addition to those women already mentioned, one might mention Katharina Schütz Zell of Strasbourg, Anne Bradstreet of New England, and more recently, Suzanne de Dietrich, Nelle Morton, Rachel Henderlite, Annie Jiagge, Margaret Towner, Sara Bernice Moseley, and Letty Russell, to name but a few.

So, yes, the Reformed tradition is known for its intellectual rigor, its passion for truth, its concern for justice, and its love of liberty. But having said all that, we must also note that prayer has been an undergirding power beneath all the achievements, the sacrifices made, the faithfulness to which the heroic figures mentioned here have borne witness.

As catholic Christians whose participation in the ecumenical movement has been another characteristic of the tradition, Reformed Christians share the heritage of prayer that is common to all Christians and they have borrowed freely from ecumenical partners. John Calvin never intended to separate completely from the church catholic, but rather to reform it and restore it to its original purity. Reformed prayer forms have adopted medieval methods, from mental prayer to lectio divina, without embarrassment. The ways Reformed Christians pray are as varied as those of Christians everywhere and include every known form of prayer practiced within Christianity.

John Calvin, like the other early reformers, was concerned that prayers for public worship be theologically sound. He therefore required that the pastors of Geneva read their prayers, often from manuscripts provided by him. This concern was rooted in anxiety about the low level of education of these early pastors. The practice of read prayers remained normative until the protest of Pietism and Puritanism. These reactions against formality came to see spontaneity as a spiritual virtue and a sign of the inspiration of the Holy Spirit. In nations where Pietism and Puritanism did not dominate, such as France and Hungary, written prayers remained the norm. Elsewhere, however, the influence of these two movements has been so pervasive that spontaneous prayer became normative for many Reformed Protestants and read prayers were strongly suspect. Extemporaneous prayer is an expression of a moment in time; it is dependent upon the feelings; it is not meant to be eloquent so much as sincere. Because this form of prayer is very common in the Reformed tradition, efforts to collect written prayers will always be incomplete. For example, we were unable to locate a single prayer by Jonathan Edwards. Only written prayers can be collected, the others vanish as they are spoken.

It has sometimes been said that Reformed people pray as if everything depends upon God, and live as if everything depends upon them.[2] Calvin expressed something of this idea himself when he wrote, "For when we invoke God, we testify that we look for good from no other quarter, and that we locate our defense nowhere else; but still we ask the help of men, as far as he allows and confers on them the power of helping us."[3] The very special relationship between prayer and action has led to great misunderstanding about the nature of prayer. Some have been critical of prayer because they fear that prayer encourages a lack of will to change what is wrong in the world. These people see prayer as a distraction from the necessary work of Christian discipleship, as a flight into otherworldliness. In fact, there is nothing passive about those who pray passionately. A great many Christians pray with faith in God and they exert great energy in their efforts to accomplish certain purposes, and they do both of these at the same time. Reformed Christians are justly known for their deeds, but their prayers are just as profound a characteristic of their piety. There have been times when the doers and the pray-ers have seen each other as sub-Christian enemies. Conflict between the two parties was particularly obvious in pre–Civil War America and could be seen during the decades of the 1950s and 1960s also. Both sides have been wrong. Prayer without action and action as a substitute for prayer are both wrong. Prayer and action belong together in the life of the believer.

As we look at Reformed prayers through the centuries, it is possible to see the influence of Puritanism and its continental equivalent, Pietism. Both protested against excessive pressure to be correct theologically. Both insisted that there was a place for the emotions in prayer. Thus, although some Reformed prayers feel more like theological essays than prayers, many other prayers display great passion, especially among the Pietists and Puritans and their heirs and followers in later periods. The "warm heart" is not alien to the Reformed tradition. The depth of feeling in these prayers communicates an intense sense of God's presence that, at times, becomes mystical.

What makes a prayer Reformed? Reformed Christians cannot be made to fit a mold. They are diverse in theology, culture, language forms, and styles of prayer; their prayers range from elegant, precise theological affirmations and the beautiful language of a prayer book, to the colloquial, extemporaneous expressions of the warmed heart. At times their variety may seem so great that it would appear they have nothing in common. Yet certain characteristics are common to Reformed prayers throughout the centuries. These commonalities should in no way be understood to mean that Reformed Christians have a corner on any of these characteristics; they are shared with all Christians. What is unique is the way in which they are combined in this tradition.

Prayer among Reformed Christians is biblical; it is shaped by the language and the instruction of scripture. As a "people of the book," Reformed Protestants know the Bible and have permitted the idiom of scripture to penetrate into their very being. This means that their prayers are filled with biblical quotations and allusions, and that metaphors absorbed from scripture are also present. To read these prayers is to feel the cadence of scripture. The prayers in this collection share this characteristic, no matter the century from which they come. Reformed Protestants use the Bible as the true measure for all prayer. They pray in the words of the Bible and they pray in the form of scripture, especially the Psalms, which, throughout the centuries, became both the hymnal and the prayerbook for Reformed Christians.

Many Reformed prayers are really expositions of the Psalms in personal form. Calvin believed that the Psalter was intended for the prayers of the people in worship and was meant to be sung. In the preface to his commentary on the Psalms, Calvin called the Psalms "an anatomy of all parts of the soul."[4] This is an apt name for them because nowhere in scripture is the variety of human emotions more clearly expressed. The Psalms become not only God's word to us but God's word with us and our word to God. They express nearly every human emotion; and thus give us permission to own our feelings. We can be angry at God because the Psalms express that kind of anger. A primary reason for the continuing popularity of the Psalms is to be found in their continuing expression of the universal emotions of people everywhere.

Because the custom was to sing the Psalms, with their wide range of emotions, Reformed people expressed their faith in ways that were quite realistic. They did not need to pretend that all was well, because the Psalms enabled them to express the fullness of all that they felt and thought. Using the Psalms in worship enabled Reformed Christians to commit many psalms to memory, and thus they were able to pray them. Isaac Watts who was an English Nonconformist and probably the most important hymn writer in the English language, took the Psalms as the basis for his hymns and rewrote them to become Christian hymns. In so doing he broke with the fixed custom of singing only the Psalms. His hymns of human composure, as he called them, continue to exercise tremendous influence on Reformed music and worship. The newest hymnals of the various Reformed denominations include a sung Psalter—a sign that the Psalms continue to exercise great influence.

Perhaps because of their Calvinist theological heritage, Reformed Christians tend to be realistic, if not pessimistic, about the human condition. As a part of the exercise of self-examination, prayer is a way to gain perspective. Confession is a consistent emphasis in these prayers from Calvin to contemporary feminists. As Reformed Christians reflect before God on their own situation, they express their shame and sense of guilt at what they see inside themselves and around them in the world. This confessional attitude includes a sense of corporate sin; the Reformed tradition has never made a clear distinction between private and public sin. As a result, confession sometimes becomes quite political in tone as the sins of monarchs and nations are laid before the divine throne.

Reformed theology has also contributed to these prayers a sense of awe and reverence in the presence of God. Although in Christ there is intimacy with God, there is also a sense of the tremendous transcendence of a God who cannot be reduced, managed, or manipulated by us. To approach the presence of God is a holy experience that is never trivial or matter-of-fact.

Another characteristic of Reformed prayer that owes a debt to Reformed theology is an appreciation of the complexity and ambiguity of life. Reformed prayers express an awareness of the difficulty of finding easy answers; they hold before God the confusions of life and the acknowledgment that only God knows the answers to some human questions. Reformed prayers seem able to live with contradiction because of a deep, abiding trust in the God who holds together all contradictions. Because of their faith in a God magnificent enough to bear the weight of the world, Reformed Protestants can let go of the need to know.

Reformed prayers also contain a strong note of thanksgiving. Because these prayers are rooted in an appreciation of the greatness and majesty of God, they rejoice in the goodness of all that God has done. Gratitude runs throughout these prayers. God is at the center of all existence and everything depends on God. This view of God leads naturally to gratitude, especially in times of joy and gladness. In times of great difficulty, it is harder to discover reasons for gratitude, yet even then the note of thanksgiving is present. People can and do find reasons for gratitude, whatever the external situation. There is really no necessary correlation between gratitude and one's outer condition. Just as there are people who appear to be very comfortable and blessed but have no sense of gratitude, so there are others whose outward condition seems grim but whose attitude is one of tremendous joy and thankfulness. The Heidelberg Catechism puts thanksgiving at the very heart of its definition of prayer:

Q. 116. Why is prayer necessary for Christians?

A. Because it is the chief part of the gratitude which God requires of us, and because God will give his grace and Holy Spirit only to those who sincerely beseech him in prayer without ceasing, and who thank him for these gifts.[5]

Even when the prayers of Reformed Christians are personal, they are expressed in corporate and communal language. A deep suspicion of the purely private life pervades Reformed theology, even though it can be said that the tradition also helped to contribute to the privatization of life. The high level of literacy that the Reformed tradition fostered was, itself, a contributing factor in the development of individualism. The suspicion of individualism may be, in part, a reaction against something which Reformed people recognize in themselves. The prayers in this collection are most often expressed in plural forms; they are the people praying together. Many were written for one of two corporate situations: the congregation or the family. These have been the two primary settings for corporate prayer throughout the centuries of Reformed history.

Reformed people pray because they share with all other Christians an appreciation of the naturalness of prayer. Prayer is something people do, almost without thought. People pray when they can do nothing else. In times of great exhilaration, they pray prayers of thanksgiving; in times of stress and turmoil, they pray prayers of petition; in times of self-examination, they pray prayers of confession. In his classic book on prayer, Harry Emerson Fosdick says, "In some form or other, it [prayer] is found everywhere, in all ages and among all peoples. The most discouraging circumstances do not crush it, and theories of the universe directly antagonistic do not prevent it."[6]

At the heart of the Christian life is the practice of regular communion with God in which prayer is the primary medium. We speak to God about what matters most to us. In this opening of our hearts, we also discover the presence of a God who cares about us. Reformed Protestants have consistently grounded their piety in the practice of prayer. One of the great saints of the Reformed tradition was John Bunyan, author of *The Pilgrim's Progress*. In his treatise on prayer, he suggested seven qualities necessary for prayer: Prayer must include sincerity, sensibility, and an affectionate pouring out of the soul. It must be offered by the strength and assistance of the Holy Spirit; offered for those things which God has promised, according to scriptures; offered for the good of the church; and offered with submission in faith to the will of God.[7] Each of these qualities points to a major characteristic of Reformed prayers: they are from the heart but also from the mind; they are offered with attention to scripture, and they are offered with a sense of the graciousness of God.

A Word about This Book

In this collection of prayers, the word "Reformed" is used in its broadest sense. It includes those Protestants on the European Continent who call themselves "Reformed," as in the usage among the Dutch, French, Swiss, Germans, and Hungarians. It includes Presbyterians from Scotland and Ireland, but it also includes persons from those denominations originating in Great Britain or America which are heirs of Puritanism and define themselves by doctrine or practice such as "Presbyterian," "Congregationalist," "Disciples of Christ," or "Baptist." We have, for example, included prayers from Walter Rauschenbusch and Harry Emerson Fosdick, who were both Baptists with strong Calvinist piety. Emily Dickinson is included although she reacted against her strict Calvinist upbringing. In spite of their differences, all of these Protestants share a devotional and theological heritage that expresses itself in a piety or spirituality which seeks to be balanced between the extremes of emotion and cold reason; between trust in God and confidence in the role that people play in God's plan; between the private soul and the community of faith.

The language of the original authors has been retained in their prayers. At times the lack of inclusive language may be uncomfortable for the contemporary reader. Still, to wrest these prayers from their cultural context would deprive them of some of their savor and would not be honest with those who read them today. Whenever we have done the translation ourselves, however, we have tried to use inclusive language.

Similarly the use of "thee" and "thou" in addressing the deity has generally been retained or incorporated in prayers written before the twentieth century. "Thee," "thy," and "thou" were the common English usage in addressing God until the middle of the twentieth century. When the New Revised Standard Version of the Bible appeared in 1989, it sanctioned by example the shift to "you," which has been occurring gradually over several decades. Unless inhibited by copyright law, we have used "you" in prayers from the twentieth century. However, copyrighted material has not been altered in the prayers from this or any other century. Most of the sources cited have used modern spelling and capitalization to assure intelligibility.

A primary source for this collection that deserves special mention is *La tradition calvinienne*, edited by Roger Chapal and Jean Pellegrin, in the series "Prières de tous les temps."[8] Designed to catch the flavor of Calvinist spirituality, as one volume in a series that includes more than two dozen collections of prayers from Christian and other traditions, this small collection draws mostly on prayers in the French language but includes translations into French from English, German, and Dutch sources. In fact, this book has inspired us to compile this collection in English exemplifying the richness of Reformed spirituality in this and several other languages and cultures. Prayers have been translated from the French by Lamar Williamson.

American Protestants from various Reformed denominations will find here prayers from their roots in the sixteenth through the nineteenth centuries. They will also discover prayers from the offshoots of this tradition in the twentieth century. All these prayers reflect a common sense of belonging to one branch of the family of Christian faith. What better way to meet relatives, some for the first time, than in the presence of God? And how better to be brought near to the throne of God than by members of one's own family?

It is our hope that readers will be inspired to a new appreciation of the piety of this heritage. To that end, we have added a concluding section of biographical material. We believe that readers will be encouraged in their own prayer life, that the power of these prayers will serve to invite the readers to learn more about some of their fellow pilgrims who are unknown, and that some of these prayers may find their way into the corporate worship of congregations and thereby enrich that worship.

The prayers are collected by century. A very brief introduction pre-
cedes the prayers of each century in which we identify the authors.
The prayers then follow. Because the twentieth century includes so
many prayers, it has been divided into three parts: (1) the twentieth
century itself, which includes prayers written by people who have
lived and died in the twentieth century, (2) prayers that anticipate the
twenty-first century because the authors are still writing as we move
toward the new millennium, and (3) prayers that have been taken
from modern service books from a variety of denominational sources
within the Reformed family. These prayers demonstrate the importance of the liturgical movement for Reformed Protestants.

All introductions, including this one, are primarily the work of
Howard Rice.

Readers may be disappointed by omissions from this collection. In
some cases, a diligent search failed to find the desired material, either
because the person in question left no written prayers or because those
that exist were not accessible to the editors. Other omissions are due to
the limitations of space, or to the limited knowledge, competence, and
perspective of the editors—limitations that they, as heirs of Calvin, do
not hesitate to acknowledge. If, in the providence of God, the deficiencies of the present work should move others to further research in
the field of Reformed prayer and piety, *soli Deo gloria!*

NOTES

1. The Westminster Shorter Catechism, in the *Book of Confessions* (Presbyterian
Church (U.S.A.), 1991), 7.098.
2. The idea is older than the Reformation. It is even older than Christianity and
has been attributed to Euripides.
3. John Calvin, Catechism of the Church of Geneva, in *Calvin: Theological Treatises*, trans. J.K.S. Reid (Philadelphia: Westminster Press, 1954), 119.
4. John Calvin, *Commentary on the Psalms*, trans. James Anderson (Grand
Rapids: Baker Book House, 1984), xxxvii.
5. The Heidelberg Catechism, in the *Book of Confessions*, 4.116.
6. Harry Emerson Fosdick, *The Meaning of Prayer* (1915; Nashville: Abingdon
Press, 1949), 9.
7. John Bunyan, "I will Pray with the Spirit" in *The Doctrine of the Law and Grace
unfolded and I will Pray with the Spirit*, ed. Richard L. Greaves (Oxford: Clarendon
Press, 1976), 236.
8. Chambray, France: Editions C.L.D. (Cahiers du Livre et du Disque), 1981.

◎ The
Sixteenth Century

The sixteenth century is the century of the giants of the Reformation. The century was marked by terrible conflict, particularly as the forces of the Counter-Reformation succeeded in driving out the Reformation from parts of Europe. The prayers of this period reflect the intensity of feeling that characterized the lives of those who lived through the wars, experienced the persecutions, yet dared to think in new and dangerous ways. The Swiss Reformation began with the preaching of John Oecolampadius (1482–1531), the leader of the Reformation in Basel, and his colleague and contemporary Ulrich Zwingli (1484–1531), the reformer in Zurich. These two set a tone for later Reformed pastoral theologians. Although they differed in their theology of the Lord's Supper, they were able to work together to begin the Swiss Reformation.

Each of the authors cited in this section played an important part in the Reformation. Another first-generation reformer was William Farel (1489–1565), who began the work in Geneva and challenged Calvin to take up his work there. Martin Bucer (1491–1551) led the Reformation in Strasbourg and welcomed Calvin there after he had been expelled from Geneva by the City Council. Marguerite of Navarre (1492–1549), a gifted poet in her own right, was a protector of Protestants when she became queen of that small kingdom. Clément Marot (1497–1544) was a poet in the court of Francis I of France. He openly avowed Protestant doctrines and Calvin invited him to put the Psalms into meter so that they could be sung. His poetic paraphrases are still sung by Reformed people across the world. Peter Martyr Vermigli (1500-1562), who was one of the great biblical scholars of the Reformation, taught in Strasbourg, then moved to England and taught at Oxford. He wrote prayers for each of the Psalms, which became very popular among Reformed people. Heinrich Bullinger (1504–1575), chief pastor of the Zurich church from the death of Zwingli until his own, was sole author of the Second Helvetic Confession. His vast correspondence and published sermons played a greater role in shaping Reformed Protestantism than is generally recognized today. John Calvin (1509–1564) was the central figure of the Reformed branch of Protestantism, and his influence on his contemporaries and on generations who followed him is without equal. The nickname "Calvinist" was commonly applied to Presbyterians, Congregationalists, Baptists, and others, including many Anglicans who owed their theological point of view to Calvin's genius. Calvin's prayers were carefully preserved by the scribe(s) who recorded his sermons.

One of Calvin's best-known pupils was John Knox (c. 1514–1572), who escaped the purges of Mary Tudor by fleeing to Geneva where he came under Calvin's influence. Upon his return to Scotland, he became a leading figure of the Reformation there. Giulio Cesare Paschali (fl. 1557), a member of the Italian-speaking evangelical community in Geneva, translated Calvin's *Institutes* and portions of the Bible into Italian. Pierre Viret (1511–1571), the great preacher of Lausanne, was also a scholar and political thinker who advocated religious freedom and separation of church and state long before these ideas were popular. Theodore Beza (1519–1605) was Calvin's successor in Geneva and, depending on one's point of view, is often credited or blamed for the beginning of Calvinist scholasticism.

By the second half of the sixteenth century, the Reformed church was well established in many parts of Europe. Also included in this section are prayers that appeared in the service books of Reformed denominations in different countries in this period: Switzerland, Holland, Scotland, Hungary, and Moravia (now a part of the Czech Republic). These formal liturgical prayers give us a sense of how our spiritual ancestors worshiped.

The prayers of these people are passionate. Their deeply held convictions shine through their piety: they believe in a God who is far above them, a God whose providential care extends to the farthest corners of earth, whose grace includes those who have in no way deserved that grace. They know human nature and are not very optimistic about human potential; their sense of sin is almost overwhelming. Were it not for the mercy of God revealed in Jesus Christ, the human situation would be hopeless. Because of their faith, however, their prayers are filled with hope, no matter how dark things seem to be. The Psalms are central to their prayers partly because the psalmist spoke of situations of trouble, persecution, and struggle not unlike their own.

The Reformation
Confession of Sins
(1525)

Heavenly Father, merciful and everlasting God, we acknowledge and confess before Thy Divine Majesty that we are poor
miserable sinners, conceived and brought forth in sin and corruption. We are prone to all evil. We cannot, without Thee, do
anything that is good. And we daily, and in many ways, trans-
gress Thy holy commandments. Thereby we provoke Thine anger
against us, and draw down upon ourselves, by Thy just judgments, death and destruction.

But, O Lord, we repent and are sorry from our hearts that we
have so displeased Thee. We condemn ourselves and our misdo-
ings, and pray that Thy grace may bring help to our distress and
misery.

Be pleased, therefore, to have mercy upon us, O most gracious
God and Father. Forgive us all our sins, through the holy sufferings of Thy dear Son, our Lord Jesus Christ. Forgive us our sins;
and grant us now the gifts of Thy Holy Spirit. Increase these in us
from day to day; so that we, acknowledging with our whole
hearts our own unrighteousness, may truly repent us of the
same; that sin may be destroyed in us; and that we may bring
forth the fruits of righteousness and a pure life which are well
pleasing unto Thee, through Jesus Christ, Amen.

Attributed to JOHN OECOLAMPADIUS (1482–1531). This prayer appears in the liturgy of
the Reformed Church of Zurich in 1525. It is sometimes attributed to Martin Bucer and
was also adapted and used by John Calvin.
From Church of Scotland, *A New Directory for the Public Worship of God* (1898), 33.

In the Midst of an Illness

Console me, Lord God, console me!
The illness increases,
Pain and fear seize
My soul and body.
Come to me then,
With Thy grace, O my only consolation!
It will surely save
Everyone, who
His Heart's desire
And hopes sets
On Thee, and who besides
Despises all gain and loss.
Now all is up,
My tongue is dumb,
It cannot speak a word.
My senses are all blighted.
Therefore is it time
That Thou my fight
Conductest hereafter
Since I am not
So strong, that I
Can bravely
Make resistance
To the Devil's wiles and treacherous hand.
Still will my spirit
Constantly abide by Thee, however he rages.

ULRICH ZWINGLI (1484–1531). Written in 1519 during a serious illness; Zwingli's most
  successful poetry.
From *Ulrich Zwingli: Early Writings*, edited by Samuel M. Jackson (reprint, Grand Rapids: Labyrinth Press,
  Baker Book House, 1987), 57.

The Bread of Thy Word

Eternal God and merciful Father, thou hast said by the sacred mouth of thy Son that those who are thirsty may come to thee and drink, that thou givest the water of life, and that thou art the bread of life that came down from heaven. Thou hast promised us that all we ask for in thy name we shall receive. Thou tellest us that as often as anyone calls on thee, thou wilt answer, and that when anyone cries to thee, thou wilt say, "Here I am." We are crying, O Lord, out of hunger. . . .

Open to us the door of thy mercy, O Savior, and tarry not so long among those near thee, and with whom thou art pleased, that thou dost not also notice us who by our iniquities displease thee. Give us the bread of thy word. And although we are ever so much worse than dogs toward thee—so far are we from being taken as thy children if one considers only us and what comes from us—thou nevertheless makest thy sun rise on the good and on the wicked, Lord, and sendest the rain on the just and the unjust. Won't these poor dogs get some crumb of bread which drops from the children's table? . . .

WILLIAM FAREL (1489–1565)
From Chapal and Pellegrin, *La tradition calvinienne*, 34. © Editions C.L.D. 1981. Used by permission.

For Children

... And so that we may effectively teach our children thy holy doctrine in reverent fear and in true and lively faith, grant that they may be given correct instruction as in the earliest church. Grant that pastors, having the care not only of adults in general and in particular but also of the children, may instruct them in the pure doctrine of faith and of all that pertains to faith, and that all these things may be carried out as they should be. Let there be in thy church correction, admonition, reception, and rejection. May thy word have there the place that belongs to it, and may true use be made of [the power of] the keys. Let schools and holy exercises to confirm thy teaching be reverently established and maintained.... Lord, let us acknowledge how thou hast worked, and may all honor and glory be given to thee.... Grant us this grace and continue and maintain it to the end, toward us and toward our loved ones....

WILLIAM FAREL (1489–1565)
From Chapal and Pellegrin, *La tradition calvinienne*, 35. © Editions C.L.D. 1981. Used by permission.

Before the Study of the Word

Eternal God, gracious Father: Thy will is that we gather in thy name to hold pious assemblies, and that we institute schools among thy people in which thy law and doctrine may be preserved and propagated. Grant thy help to us who are gathered here in thy name, so that all we say or do may serve to make thy glory known and contribute to the good of thy church. Through thy Son, our Savior Jesus Christ, who lives and reigns with thee in the unity of the Holy Spirit, forever and ever. Amen.

MARTIN BUCER (1491–1551). Bucer often recited this prayer before his lectures at Cambridge, 1549.
From Chapal and Pellegrin, *La tradition calvinienne*, 33. © Editions C.L.D. 1981. Used by permission.

All My Salvation
Lies in Thee

Alas, O God, save me, I cry.
What will become of me?
No good I see within myself;
All good must come from Thee.

All my salvation lies in Thee;
Without Thee I am lost.
I know the law which for my sin
Would have me pay the cost.

So grant me, Lord, both grace and faith
To shield my troubled soul.
Alone, we're less than naught, unless
It please thee to uphold.

Thou art my All, I know it well,
By thee let me be sought;
Extract me from this cluttered life
In which thou seest me caught.

Oh, pay the debt I owe, and then
To Thine own self join me.
Alas, O God, save me, I cry.
What will become of me?

MARGUERITE OF NAVARRE (1492–1549)

From Chapal and Pellegrin, *La tradition calvinienne*, 39. © Editions C.L.D. 1981. Used by permission.

Psalm 130

From the depth of my mind,
The abyss of my care,
Unto thee day and night
Do I cry out in prayer.

It is time now, O Lord,
My complaints all to hear.
I am urgent in word;
To my voice do give ear.

If our sins should receive
The full force of thy hand,
Who among us, O Lord,
Before thee could stand?

But thou art not severe;
Thou art quick to show grace.
That is why we revere
Both thy Law and thy face.

I find solace in God;
My soul counts on the Lord,
And I place all my hope
In the strength of his word.

My soul looks to God
Always and without stay,
More than guards watch for dawn
At the breaking of day.

Of Israel's hope
Let the Lord be the ground,
For in him there is help;
Yes, in God grace abounds.

He it is without doubt
Who keeps Israel from sin
And from all of her faults
Will redeem at the end.

CLÉMENT MAROT (1497–1544)

From Chapal and Pellegrin, *La tradition calvinienne*, 36–37. © Editions C.L.D. 1981. Used by permission.

Prayer from Psalm 46

Your help was always at hand, O great and good God, for those in affliction who believe truly that you are their only protection and strength. Your faithful are therefore delivered from fear, even if the whole earth is shaken, the mountains waver, the waves and surging of the sea pound the shore so strongly that it seems that everything is about to collapse into the water and float away. Your people, in contrast, are gifted with supreme confidence because in the midst of their troubles you refresh them with pleasant streams of consolation by your fruitful Spirit and by putting forth rare and wonderful proofs of your help. We rely on your goodness and, despite our countless sins by which we confess that we have seriously offended you, we pray that the nations and kingdoms, which you see attacking your Church with great force and sly plots, may themselves waver and grow weak. May you cry out with that voice of yours which is wont to shake and break up the earth and all creatures. May you, our God, stand by us like a fortified citadel. Take away wars. May spears, horses, chariots, and all kinds of weapons grow weak without you so that those who are attacking us may finally give up their efforts. May you appear sublime and exalted before all creatures, after you have been acclaimed for providing us better protection than all the armies and all the power of this world. Through Jesus Christ, our Lord. Amen.

PETER MARTYR VERMIGLI (1500–1562)

From Peter Martyr Vermigli, *Sacred Prayers Drawn from the Psalms of David*, edited by John P. Donnelly and Joseph McLelland (Kirksville, Mo.: Sixteenth Century Journal Publications, 1996), 45. Used by permission of the publisher.

Prayer from Psalm 130

O Almighty God, you have been accustomed to afflict your faithful harshly and rather often so that thereby they may return to you with burning and perfect repentance. This is what we are experiencing in the Church now in these trouble-filled times, for we, who hitherto have been ungrateful to you in countless ways and who have everywhere transgressed your commandments and law, have been so harassed innumerable times by the fierceness of the devil and his minions that we are forced to cry out to you from the abyss and the deepest depths of our misfortunes lest you were to wish to punish our sins so severely. If you decided, O God, both to examine and to punish our iniquities according to their merits, who of us would be so clean and holy that he would stand before your justice? But because we know that you are noteworthy for your supreme kindness, each morning and evening we look up and wait for your help. So despite the fact that our iniquities are very numerous, may you be pleased to redeem us from them all out of your abundant goodness and mercy so that, freed from present dangers and pressing troubles, we may both believe and proclaim that true redemption is found in you alone. Through Jesus Christ our Lord. Amen.

PETER MARTYR VERMIGLI (1500–1562)

From Peter Martyr Vermigli, *Sacred Prayers Drawn from the Psalms of David*, edited by John P. Donnelly and Joseph McLelland (Kirksville, Mo.: Sixteenth Century Journal Publications, 1996), 142. Used by permission of the publisher.

Morning Prayer
for Young Students

Lord almighty, eternal and merciful God, Father, Son, and Holy Spirit: we pray to you and adore you with all our heart as our only true Lord, God, Creator and Father. We confess that you are the only, highest, and best good, the almighty creator of heaven and of earth, the mighty Triune Lord, ruler and sustainer of all creatures.

We laud and praise you as the true, just, gracious, and merciful God, and we call out to you about all our needs of soul and body, but especially that we may truly be able to believe, pray, ponder and think, do and leave undone. And we give you great praise and thanks that through this night you have kept us so mercifully. And [we] pray with all our hearts that you would graciously keep us this day from sin, shame, wickedness, and from all evil.

May you give us also your Holy Spirit, through whose mercy we are being prepared to teach: to learn all that is right and good and to keep what we need most and for which we are being educated, so that in time we become faithful servants of you and of the government which creates much good in the world and brings pleasant fruit.

O Lord, be gracious to all who teach us and keep us, especially toward our lords and masters. Uphold them through your grace, grant that they may rule with wisdom, justice, mercy, and courage over city and country, to protect and shield and keep us in peace and prosperity, so that we may serve you always and be thankful to you for all our good things, through Jesus Christ our Lord. Amen.

HEINRICH BULLINGER (1504–1575)

From *Small Christian Prayerbook* (in German), 52–54. Translated by Cornelia Cyss-Wittenstein.

Concerning Keeping One's Good Name against the Wagging of Bad Tongues

Heavenly Father, you have taught us through the wise king Solomon that a good name is more precious than all riches, goodwill better than silver and gold [Prov. 22]. Yet such a good name we cannot receive or keep without your special help, protection, and shield against false and bad tongues. And you have also shown us the means through which we may draw from the fountain and origin of a good name and receive one, namely that we live blamelessly.

Thus grant me now that I may conduct myself guiltlessly throughout all my life, so that nobody can accuse me of wickedness. Instead, may all people always keep in front of them the saying of Samuel, the judge, "Can anyone among you say that I have used force or committed an injustice against anyone?" [1 Sam. 12].

Yet even the upright and innocent are not safe from envious and conspiring people, who carry hidden among their vices the poison of adders; so that it often happens we believe we are among good and trusted friends and instead live among scorpions as did the holy prophet Ezekiel [chap. 2]. And just as King David laments [Ps. 27], there are many evil tongues against me. . . . Therefore I, too, call and cry out in my need and affliction to God the Lord and he does not stop up his ears. Lord, do hear me graciously, for the mouths of the people are lying and the tongues are false and flattering. Save my life from great danger and keep it graciously through your mercy [Ps. 120].

But if, O Lord, it pleases you according to your just law and judgment to sustain me through these evil tongues [in order to attain] humility and greater piety, then also grant me graciously that with the holy Paul [2 Cor. 6] I may experience in my heart, in honor and shame, throughout bad and good repute, patience in your commandments, your pleasure and will, through our Lord Jesus Christ. Amen.

HEINRICH BULLINGER (1504–1575)
From *Small Christian Prayerbook* (in German), 119. Translated by Cornelia Cyss-Wittenstein.

Morning Prayer

My God, my Father and my Savior, since it has pleased thee to preserve me by thy grace through the night just ended and until the present day, grant that I may use it entirely in thy service and that I may think, say, and do nothing but to please thee and to obey thy holy will, so that all my actions may redound to the glory of thy name and the edification of my neighbors. And just as in this earthly life thou causest the sun to shine on the world to give physical light, let thy Holy Spirit illumine my mind to guide me in the way of thy righteousness. Thus in everything I do, let my goal and intention always be to walk reverently and to honor and serve thee, relying only on thy blessing for my well-being, and undertaking only what is pleasing to thee.

Grant also, O Lord, that as I labor for my physical needs and for this present life, I may lift up my soul to that heavenly and blessed life which thou hast promised to thy children. . . . And since to begin well means little unless one perseveres, I beseech thee to be my guide not only today but for all my life, daily continuing and increasing thy grace in me until thou hast brought me into full union with thy Son, Jesus Christ our Lord, who is the true Sun of our souls, shining day and night forever. . . . Amen.

JOHN CALVIN (1509–1564)
From *Opera quae supersunt omnia*, 6:136.

Evening Prayer

Lord God, since thou hast made the night for man to rest as thou hast created the day for his work, I beseech thee to give my body a restful night and to grant that my soul may be lifted up to thee and my heart always filled with thy love.

Teach me, O God, to entrust all my cares to thee and constantly to remember thy mercy, so that my soul also may enjoy spiritual rest. Let not my sleep be excessive, but let it serve to renew my strength so I may be more ready to serve thee. May it please thee also to keep me pure in body and in spirit, preserving me from all temptations and all danger, so that my very sleep may contribute to the glory of thy name.

And since this day has not passed without my having offended thee in several ways, I who am a poor sinner make this request. Grant, O God, that just as thou hast now hid all things in the shadows of the night, thou wilt also bury all my sins in thy mercy, through Jesus Christ my Savior. Amen.

JOHN CALVIN (1509–1564)

From Chapal and Pellegrin, *La tradition calvinienne*, 26. © Editions C.L.D. 1981. Used by permission. From the Catechism of 1542.

On Approaching the Holy Table

Since by thy fatherly goodness thou dost invite us today to receive the holy testimonies of our peace and reconciliation with thee, and since thy son Jesus, who died for us, calls to himself all those who labor and are heavy laden, thou wilt surely not reject thy servant who begs thy grace and seeks salvation and life in the death of Jesus Christ. Now therefore lift my heart to thee: give me thy Holy Spirit. Grant me grace to approach this table with humble repentance and a thirsty soul that desires thy grace. Strengthen my faith so that, receiving by hand these visible signs, I may receive by faith the broken body of Jesus Christ and his blood shed for me as the nourishment of eternal life.

JOHN CALVIN (1509–1564)
From Chapal and Pellegrin, *La tradition calvinienne*, 27. © Editions C.L.D. 1981. Used by permission.

A Prayer for School Children

O Lord, source of all wisdom and knowledge, since it pleases thee to provide me during my youth with the education I need to lead a holy and honest life, enlighten also my intelligence so that I may understand the instruction I am given. . . .

And since thou dost promise to enlighten by thy wisdom and knowledge the upright in heart who are little and humble, while thou rejectest the proud so they get lost in their vain reasoning, I ask thee, O my God, to create in me the true humility that will make me teachable and obedient, first of all to thee, but also to those whom thou hast appointed to teach me. Grant at the same time that, having renounced all evil desires, my heart may seek thee ardently and that my only goal, O God, may be to prepare myself from this time forward to serve thee in the vocation to which it will please thee to call me.

JOHN CALVIN (1509–1564). From the Latin edition of Calvin's Catechism, 1545.
From Chapal and Pellegrin, *La tradition calvinienne*, 28. © Editions C.L.D. 1981. Used by permission.

Since Thou Hast Chosen Us to Serve Thee

Almighty God, thou hast seen fit to take us to be thy priests, and hast chosen us while we were not only in a lowly condition but even profane and strangers to all holiness, and hast dedicated us to thyself by thy Holy Spirit. Grant now that we may offer ourselves to thee as a holy sacrifice.

O let us remember thy charge and call. Let us consecrate ourselves to thy service and so present to thee our effort and our labor. May thy Name really be glorified in us and may our ingrafting into the Body of thine only Son be truly evident. As he is the chief and sole and eternal Priest, grant us to become participants in this priesthood with which thou hast chosen to honor him, so that he may take us as his own associates. Thus may thy Name perpetually be praised by the entire Body as well as by its Head.

JOHN CALVIN (1509–1564). From a lecture on Malachi 1:9.
From Chapal and Pellegrin, *La tradition calvinienne*, 29. © Editions C.L.D. 1981. Used by permission.

Morning Prayer
with the City Guard

(The first lines of this text follow, almost word for word, Calvin's Morning Prayer, above.)

And since, O Heavenly Father, the inhabitants and sojourners in this city, after thee, rely on the fidelity and foresight of us who are members of the guard, grant us grace so to carry out our duty that no mishap may occur here due to our carelessness or negligence. And most of all may it please thee, O mighty God of armies, to transform this miserable time of calamity into a happy time in which piety and justice reign, so that we may no longer have the trouble of standing guard.

Finally we beseech thee, most merciful God, to give thy Holy Spirit and the knowledge of thee to all people, instituting and always maintaining among us good and faithful pastors. . . .

All these things we ask thee, gracious God and Father, in the name and for the sake of our Savior, Jesus Christ.

ANONYMOUS; Sancerre, France (1573). Sancerre, a city in central France, was a Protestant stronghold during the sixteenth-century wars of religion.

From Chapal and Pellegrin, *La tradition calvinienne*, 44. © Editions C.L.D. 1981. Used by permission.

For Christ's Flock

O God of all power, Who hast called from death the great Pastor of the sheep, our Lord Jesus, comfort and defend the flock which He hath redeemed by the blood of the eternal testament; increase the number of true preachers; mitigate and lighten the hearts of the ignorant; relieve the pains of such as be afflicted, but especially of those that suffer for the testimony of the Truth, by the power of our Lord Jesus Christ. Amen.

JOHN KNOX (c. 1514–1572)
From Selina F. Fox, *A Chain of Prayer across the Ages* (New York: E. P. Dutton & Co., 1943), 174.

A Sabbath Prayer of Thanksgiving

Honour and praise be unto you, O Lord our God, for all your tender mercies again bestowed upon us throughout another week.

Continual thanks be unto you for creating us in your own likeness; for redeeming us by the precious blood of your dear Son when we were lost; and for sanctifying us with the Holy Spirit.

For your help and succour in our necessities, your protection in many dangers of body and soul; your comfort in our sorrows, and for sparing us in life, and giving us so large a time to repent. For all the benefits, O most merciful Father, that we have received of your goodness alone, we thank you; and we beseech you to grant us always your Holy Spirit, that we may grow in grace, in steadfast faith, and perseverance in all good works, through Jesus Christ our Lord.

JOHN KNOX (c. 1514–1572)
From Mary Bachelor, ed., *The Lion's Prayers Collection*, 44. Oxford: Lion Publishing Co., 1992.

To Eat and Drink
at His Table

O Lord, we acknowledge that no creature is able to comprehend the length and breadth, the deepness and height, of that thy most excellent love, which moved thee to show mercy where none was deserved; to promise and give life where death had gotten victory; to receive us into thy grace when we could do nothing but rebel against thy justice.

O Lord, the blind dullness of our corrupt nature will not suffer us sufficiently to weigh these thy most ample benefits; yet, nevertheless, at the commandment of Jesus Christ our Lord, we present ourselves to this his Table (which he hath left to be used in remembrance of his death until his coming again) to declare and witness before the world that by him alone we have entrance to the throne of thy grace; that by him alone we are possessed in our spiritual kingdom, to eat and drink at his Table; with whom we have our conversation presently in heaven; and by whom our bodies shall be raised up again from the dust, and shall be placed with him in that endless joy which thou, O Father of mercy, hast prepared for thine elect, before the foundation of the world was laid.

JOHN KNOX (c. 1514–1572)

From David Laing, ed., *The Works of John Knox* (Edinburgh: James Thin, 1895), 4:195–96.

A Prayer Used in the Assemblies of the Church

Eternal and everliving God, Father of our Lord Jesus Christ, thou that of thine infinite goodness hast chosen to thyself a Church, unto the which ever from the fall of man thou hast manifested thyself: first, by thine own voice to Adam; next to Abraham and his seed, then to all Israel, by the publication of thy holy law; and last, by sending of thy only Son, our Lord Jesus Christ, that great Angel of thy Counsel, into this world, and clad with our nature, to teach unto us thy holy will and to put an end to all revelations and prophecies; who also elected to himself Apostles, to whom, after his Resurrection he gave commandment to publish and preach his Evangel to all realms and nations; promising to be with them even to the end of the world; yea, and moreover, that wheresoever two or three were gathered together in his Name, that he would be there in the midst of them, not only to instruct and teach them, but also to ratify and confirm such things as they shall pronounce or decree by thy Word. . . .

Give unto us, O Lord, that presently are assembled in thy Name, such abundance of thy holy Spirit, that we may see those things that shall be expedient for the advancement of thy glory, in the midst of this perverse and stubborn generation. Give us grace, O Lord, that universally amongst our selves, we may agree in the unity of true doctrine. Preserve us from damnable errors, and grant unto us such purity and cleanness of life, that we be not slanderous to thy blessed Evangel. Bless thou so our weak labors, that the fruits of the same may redound to the praise of thy holy Name, to the profit of this present generation, and of the posterity to come, through Jesus Christ our Lord; to whom, with Thee and the Holy Ghost, be all honor and praise, now and ever. So be it.

JOHN KNOX (c. 1514–1572). From the Book of Common Order.
From David Laing, ed., *The Works of John Knox* (Edinburgh: James Thin, 1895), 6: 314–16.

De Profundis

Heavenly Father, if thou shouldst take account of our sins, we all know, alas, that we are unworthy to lift our eyes toward thee. Still less dare we to hope, in the miserable condition in which we live, that from thy high throne thy benevolence should answer our desires and prayers. We well know, indeed, the gravity of all our faults.

We have wandered and strayed from thy way, carried away by our perverse desires and wild impulses. Our heart does not revere thy living Word, and our tongue refuses to praise thy benefits. It is good that today thy faithful word corrects us and exhorts us to a better life, for our proud, rebellious spirits despise thy appeals.

But thou art our sublime Father in heaven and we your children are of lowly clay. Thou art our creator and we the work of thy hands. Thou art the Shepherd and we the flock that thou hast redeemed in thy mercy. Finally, thou art the God who givest life and we the nation thou hast chosen and cherished. . . .

Do not smite us severely and, since thou art good, may thy punishment seem gentle to us.

GIULIO CESARE PASCHALI (sixteenth century)
From Chapal and Pellegrin, *La tradition calvinienne*, 40. © Editions C.L.D. 1981. Used by permission.

To Rest in Thee

Alas, Lord, we are not worthy that the earth should support us, nor worthy to set our eyes on heaven. . . . But please do not turn thy face from us; look with pity not on us but on thy Son Jesus Christ.

Grant that we shall turn to no other God but thee. Grant us to keep thy holy rest by resting from our work, in order to let thee work in us.

PIERRE VIRET (1511–1571)
From Chapal and Pellegrin, *La tradition calvinienne*, 41. © Editions C.L.D. 1981. Used by permission.

The Church of the Risen One

O gracious God Eternal, Father, Son and Holy Spirit, eternal praise be given thee because it hath pleased thee to enlighten our minds to recognize these abominations and to detest them in our hearts. In their place, grant us to live and die in the truth which thou hast sent from heaven anew, as it were, in our time. Preserve thy poor, true Church against this spirit of error, within and without.

Look not at what the world deserves, when it refuses and tries only to send back to heaven such a light. Let the knowledge of thy holy name be accompanied in us by true faith and recovery of our senses. Forget our sins and remember thy promises. Cause those whom thou hast honored with thy holy ministry to grow in all wisdom, zeal, discretion, and all the other gifts that are so necessary to reestablish thy house. . . .

Complete the number of thy elect and, putting an end to all that is opposed to thee, come soon, Lord, to stop the mouths of thine adversaries forever . . . and fully to open the mouths of thine own to praise thee eternally. Amen.

THEODORE OF BEZA (1519–1605). A prayer offered in Geneva, 1593.
From Chapal and Pellegrin, *La tradition calvinienne*, 32. © Editions C.L.D. 1981. Used by permission.

A Prayer after Communion

Almighty God, heavenly Father, we praise you and extol you, for you have again amply given us the blessed benefits of your sacraments. You have satisfied us with the food and drink of eternal life, and you have again assigned us the signs and seals of your mercy. Having been fulfilled with the benefits of your altar, we offer ourselves, our bodies and souls, as a holy, as a precious offering, that all of us who have just united with Jesus Christ and through Christ with one another, may grow daily in faith, may rejoice in hope, and may enrich ourselves in familial love. May praise, glory, honor, and thanksgiving descend upon your holy name now and forever. Amen.

HUNGARIAN REFORMED LITURGY (sixteenth century)

Adapted by László Ravasz, 1929. Reprinted from *Book of Worship* © 1986 by the United Church of Christ. Used by permission of the United Church of Christ, Office for Church Life and Leadership.

Prayers at the Explanation
of the Catechism

Before:

O heavenly Father, Thy Word is perfect, restoring the soul, making wise the simple, and enlightening the eyes of the blind, and a power of God unto salvation for every one that believes. We, however, are by nature blind and incapable of doing anything good, and Thou wilt succor only those who have a broken and contrite heart and who revere Thy Word. We beseech Thee, therefore, that Thou wilt illumine our darkened minds with Thy Holy Spirit and give us a humble heart, free from all haughtiness and carnal wisdom, in order that we, hearing Thy Word, may rightly understand it and may regulate our lives accordingly. . . .

After:

O gracious and merciful God and Father, we thank Thee that Thou hast established Thy covenant with believers and their seed. This Thou hast not only sealed by holy baptism, but Thou daily showest it by perfecting Thy praise out of the mouths of babes and sucklings, thus putting to shame the wise and prudent of this world. We beseech Thee that Thou wilt increase Thy grace in them, in order that they may unceasingly grow in Christ, Thy Son, until they have reached complete maturity in all wisdom and righteousness. Give us grace to instruct them in Thy knowledge and fear, according to Thy commandment. May by their godliness the kingdom be strengthened, unto the glory of Thy Holy Name and unto their eternal salvation, through Jesus Christ, Thy Son our Lord, who taught us to pray, saying, Our Father . . . Amen.

DUTCH PSALTER, 1566. Prayers in the Liturgy of the 1934 *Psalter Hymnal* all date from the time of the Reformation.

From Christian Reformed Church, *Psalter Hymnal* (1934), 76–77. Used by permission of CRC Publications.

Advent Prayer

Almighty God, our heavenly Father,
Thou dost faithfully fulfill Thy promises.
We thank thee that thou didst send thine only begotten Son
in the fullness of time.
With all thy church we celebrate his joyful coming.
We glorify thee, our gracious Father,
and thy Son, our King from Zion,
and the Holy Spirit.
Thou, our King, who camest in the name of thy Father, we beg thee,
enable us to celebrate thy holy advent
in our hearts, with our words, and through our devoted lives.
Pour out thy bountiful blessing upon us.
Enable us to listen to thy Word with eagerness,
to trust it and accept it in faith,
so that we may joy in thy Spirit and offer thee our adoration.
Let us serve thee, the Incarnate God, our Redeemer,
in all this time here in thy Church now,
and then in thy Kingdom for ever.
Amen.

UNITAS FRATRUM (Moravian Brethren) (sixteenth century)
Translated by Martin Prudký from Evangelical Church of Czech Brethren, *Agenda Českobratrské církve evangelické* (Liturgical Handbook), 2:366.

℘ The
Seventeenth Century

The seventeenth century was marked by the rise of Puritanism in Great Britain and Pietism on the continent of Europe. Both these movements were in part protests against the development of Protestant orthodoxy. Over against the scholastic/orthodox insistence on the centrality of right belief, both Pietists and Puritans insisted on the centrality of the experience of Christ in the human soul. No person of this period was more influential in the lives of Reformed people than Lewis Bayly (d. 1631), whose book *The Practice of Piety* had been published in seventy-one different English editions by 1792. Although he remained an Anglican, he was a Calvinist and had obvious Puritan convictions. Pierre du Moulin (1568–1658) was a professor and theologian in France, England, and the Netherlands. Richard Sibbes (1577–1635) was an early Puritan leader and teacher in both Cambridge and London. Francis Rous (1579–1659) was chaplain to Oliver Cromwell and a genuine Puritan mystic. Anne de Rohan (1584–1646) was noted for her piety among the French Reformed of the period. Jean Mestrezat (1592–1657) was a well-known preacher and apologist in France. Charles Drelincourt (1595–1669) was pastor at Charenton, France, beginning in 1650. Oliver Cromwell (1599–1658) was the Lord Protector of England during the Interregnum between Charles I and Charles II. He served as head of the nation although he fought against every effort to vest too much power in him and he sought to rule as first among equals. The Westminster Assembly (the Westminster Divines), appointed by the Long Parliament (1643–1648), produced the Westminster Confession of Faith, the Shorter and Larger Catechisms, a Form of Government, and a Directory for the Public Worship of God, from which one prayer has been included here.

The greatest poet of Puritanism was John Milton (1608–1674), who gave expression to the cry for personal experience of the risen Christ in forms that have been preserved through the centuries. Anne Bradstreet (1612–1672) did the same thing for New England Puritans. Her prayers and poems express the Puritan longing for intimacy with God, yet they also preserved her own Calvinist sense of God's transcendent glory. Richard Baxter (1615–1691) was the author of influential works that came to prominence even after the demise of Puritanism as a political force. His book *The Saints' Everlasting Rest* is deeply personal, almost mystical. No Puritan writer had as much influence as John Bunyan (1628–1688), whose book *The Pilgrim's Progress* was more widely read than any other book in English besides the Bible. Bunyan's only recorded prayer is a poetic adaptation of the Lord's Prayer. Across the Channel, Pierre Jurieu (1637–1713) was a French preacher who served as pastor of French immigrants in Rotterdam. Monsieur de Richelieu (fl. 1659) was pastor of the Reformed Church of Plouer and Saint Malo, on the north coast of Brittany. Claude Brousson (1647–1698), trained as an attorney, was a pastor among Protestants hiding from persecution in the rugged back country of southern France. He became a martyr for the faith. An important Scottish figure was Henry Scougal (1650–1678), who taught in Aberdeen. Though he died at twenty-eight, he wrote a book that expressed and shaped Reformed piety, *The Life of God in the Soul of Man*. In Hungary, Karoly Jeszensky was another minister who knew persecution, having served as a galley slave. The Camisards (1685–1704) were a Protestant resistance group in southern France after the revocation of the Edict of Nantes.

One can trace the constant theme of God's majesty in these prayers; many of the authors knew the pain of persecution and banishment. But there is also a note of a more deeply personal faith than that of the sixteenth century. These prayers weave theological affirmations with the stuff of ordinary life. They bring before God the daily events of life, trusting in God's gracious care.

A Prayer for the Morning

O most mighty and glorious God! full of incomprehensible power and majesty; whose glory the very heaven of heavens is not able to contain! Look down from heaven upon me, thine unworthy servant, who here prostrate myself at the footstool of thy throne of grace. But look upon me, O Father, through the merits and mediation of Jesus Christ, thy beloved Son, in whom only thou art well pleased! For of myself, I am not worthy to stand in thy presence, or to speak with mine unclean lips to so holy a God as thou art. For thou knowest that in sin I was conceived and born, and that I have lived ever since in iniquity; so that I have broken all thy holy commandments by sinful motions, unclean thoughts, evil words, and wicked works; omitting many of those duties which thou requirest for thy service, and committing many of those vices which thou, under the penalty of thy displeasure, hast forbidden.

And for these my sins, O Lord, I stand here guilty of thy curse, with all the miseries of this life, and everlasting torments in hellfire, when this wretched life is ended, if thou shouldst deal with me according to my deserts. Yea, Lord, I confess that it is thy mercy which endureth for ever, and thy compassion which never fails, that is the cause that I have not been long ago consumed. But with thee, O Lord, there is mercy, and plenteous redemption. In the multitude, therefore, of thy mercy, and confidence in Christ's merits, I entreat thy divine Majesty that thou wouldst not enter into judgment with thy servant. But be thou merciful unto me, and wash away all the uncleaness of my sin, with the merits of that precious blood which Jesus Christ hath shed for me.

LEWIS BAYLY (d. 1631)
From Lewis Bayly, *The Practice of Piety*, 108–9. Reprinted 1995 by Soli Deo Gloria, Morgan, Pa.

On Approaching Thy Holy Table

My God, my Father, I lift up my heart to thee. Give me thy Holy Spirit.

Grant me the grace to approach this table with humble repentance and ardent desire in Jesus Christ our Lord.

Grant me to receive this holy sacrament with firm faith in thy word, that in receiving these visible signs from thy hand I may receive by faith the body and blood of Jesus Christ, who died for me as the nourishment of eternal life.

May I take from it the peace and spiritual joy proper to thy children with ardent love for thee, my God, and a firm resolve henceforth to consecrate my life to thy service, until I see thy face and my soul is received by Jesus Christ my Savior, who has redeemed it by his death.

PIERRE DU MOULIN (1568–1658)
From Chapal and Pellegrin, *La tradition calvinienne*, 52. © Editions C.L.D. 1981. Used by permission.

For Consistent Christian Lives

Lord, Thou hast made Thyself to be ours, therefore now show Thyself to us in Thy wisdom, goodness and power. To walk faithfully in our Christian course we need much grace. Supply us out of Thy rich store. We need wisdom to go in and out inoffensively before others; furnish us with Thy Spirit. We need patience and comfort, Thou that art the God of consolations bestow it upon us; for Christ's sake. Amen.

RICHARD SIBBES (1577–1635)
From Selina F. Fox, *A Chain of Prayer across the Ages* (New York: E. P. Dutton & Co., 1943), 151.

A Song of Love

Thou hast touched my soul with thy spirit, O most beloved, and virtue is going out of thee into me, and draweth me to thee. Thy spirit is a loadstone of love and where it toucheth spirits, it leaveth love and this love makes a soul to move to her beloved that touched her. So by thee doth she run after thee, O thou fountain and rest of loves. Thy ointments draw thee, O thou anointer, her loves begin and end in thee. O let my love overrun this circle of love; let her ever be tasting of thy loves, and ever love thee by tasting them! Let the savor of thy ointments whose very breath is love, be ever in her nostrils that she may ever love thee for that savor and by it. Give me the flagons of the new wine of thy kingdom, which may lift up my soul above herself in her loves, and give her better loves than her own, wherewith to love him that is far better than herself. Yea, let her drink plentifully, that she may be mounted up in a divine ecstacy above her carnal and earthly station; that she may forget the low and base griefs and cares, and distractions of carnal and worldly love, and by a heavenly excess be transported into a heavenly love to embrace her beloved, who is the Lord from heaven, with a love that is like him.

FRANCIS ROUS (1579–1659)
From *The Mystical Marriage* (1656), 735.

On the Death of Her Mother
(1631)

After suffering so much strain,
Fear and famine, loss and grief,
Days of trouble, nights of pain,
Prison cold beyond belief,
Was it needful, Lord, that I
Should have to see my mother die?
But thou didst will it, Lord, and here
Below, thy will's our law. No fear,
Because we know thy will is just
And equitable, and we know
That thy wise goodness we can trust.
I have no need to grumble so.

Forgive, O Lord, my rash demand;
None but my holy prayers fulfill.
Do in me what thou dost command
And then command what thou dost will.
Make me to know, O God—I must—
That thou art God and I but dust.
Thou art all and I am naught,
Nor can I do the things I ought.
Thou doest good, so do drive out
The sadness that I feel within.
Let not self-pity make me pout,
But make me to deplore my sin.

Of all the good that thou hast done
The sum lies in this act of love:
Thou madest human thine own Son
To make us sons of God above.
Thy sinless child thou gavest over,

A sinful people to deliver.
The Master made himself a slave;
The Leader assumed debt, to save.
I, just a sheep, am blessed indeed—
My Shepherd's flesh I have for food,
And thou hast met thy creature's need
Washed in the great Creator's blood.

ANNE DE ROHAN (1584–1646)
From Chapal and Pellegrin, *La tradition calvinienne*, 46–47. © Editions C.L.D. 1981. Used by permission.

After the Lord's Supper

O my God, enlighten more and more the eyes of my understanding so that I may grasp what is the height and depth, the
length and breadth of thy love toward us.

What depth, that thou hast pulled us out of the chasm of death
by the death of thy Son!

What height, that thou dost raise us by him and with him to
the heavenly places!

What length is the eternal duration forever and ever of the
bliss thou hast prepared for us!

What breadth, that thou removest our sins from us as far as the
east is from the west, and that however many may be thy blessings and promises, they are Yes and Amen in Jesus Christ.

O God, thou allowest me to see such marvelous goodness and
hast spread it before my eyes in the sacrament I have just received. Grant me to contemplate that goodness with such delight
that I may be transformed into the image of thine own graciousness and may be all love toward thee. . . .

JEAN MESTREZAT (1592–1657)
From Chapal and Pellegrin, *La tradition calvinienne*, 51. © Editions C.L.D. 1981. Used by permission.

Prayer of a Sufferer
Preparing to Die

O great God! I know that thou canst do anything, and that thou art the one who makest the wound and who bindest it up. Thou dost afflict and thy hand healeth; thou bringest down to the grave and thou bringest back. Thou healest, when thou wilt, the most desperately ill and thou bringest back to life and callest into being things that are not, as if they were.

O matchless physician, not only canst thou pour out thy blessing on the remedies given to me; thou hast but to say the word and I shall be perfectly whole.

If, though, for thine own reasons, thou dost wish my illness to continue, sustain me, Lord, and redouble thy fatherly care and the consolation of thy Spirit. Arm me with truly Christian patience and clothe me with a constancy worthy of the faith with which thou hast honored me. . . .

Long have I considered this bed as the image of the grave in which I shall soon be laid, and I think of death as the hand that will come and break the last link in this chain of misery. It is death that will deliver me from this wretched tabernacle and lead me into the glorious, incorruptible palace where thou livest and where I shall praise thee eternally. Amen.

CHARLES DRELINCOURT (1595–1669)

From Chapal and Pellegrin, *La tradition calvinienne*, 50. © Editions C.L.D. 1981. Used by permission.

Prayer for the Nation

Lord, though I am a miserable and wretched creature, I am in Covenant with you through grace. And I may, I will, come to you, for your people. You have made me, though very unworthy, a mean instrument to do them some good, and you service; and many of them have set too high a value upon me, though others wish and would be glad of my death; Lord, however you dispose of me, continue and go on to do good for them. Give them consistency of judgment, one heart, and mutual love; and go on to deliver them, and with them the work of reformation; and make the name of Christ glorious in the world. Teach those who look too much on your instruments, to depend more on yourself. Pardon such as desire to trample on the dust of such a poor worm; for they are your people too. And pardon the folly of this short prayer—even for Jesus Christ's sake. And give us a good night, if it be your pleasure.

OLIVER CROMWELL (1599–1658). Cromwell was a Puritan who served as Lord Protector of England 1653–1658.

From Horton Davies, *The Communion of Saints: Prayers of the Famous* (Grand Rapids: Wm. B. Eerdmans Publishing Co., 1990), 136.

Offering Ourselves to God

O God,
who hast so greatly loved us,
and mercifully redeemed us;
give us grace that in everything
we may yield ourselves,
our wills and our works,
a continual thankoffering unto thee;
through Jesus Christ our Lord. Amen.

THE WESTMINSTER DIVINES. Written for the Directory for Worship of 1647.
From Uniting Church in Australia, *Uniting in Worship*, 222.

Prayer for Illumination

Holy Spirit of God, who prefers before all temples the upright heart and pure, instruct us in all truth; what is dark, illumine, what is low, raise and support, what is shallow, deepen; that every chapter in our lives may witness to your power and justify the ways of God. In the name of Jesus, giver of all grace. Amen.

JOHN MILTON (1608–1674)
From H. Davies, *The Communion of Saints: Prayers of the Famous* (Grand Rapids: Wm. B. Eerdmans Publishing Co., 1990), 60.

Prayer for the Spirit

Vouchsafe to us, though unworthy, a plenteous out-pouring of Thy Spirit to refresh Thy heritage, for Thy Kingdom is now at hand, and Thou art standing at the door. Hear us, we beseech Thee, O Lord. Amen.

JOHN MILTON (1608–1674)
From Selina F. Fox, *A Chain of Prayer across the Ages* (New York: E. P. Dutton & Co., 1943), 218.

Upon My Son Samuel, His Goeing for England, November 6, 1657

Thou mighty God of Sea and Land,
I here resigne into thy hand
The Son of Prayers, of vowes, of teares,
The child I stay'd for many yeares,
Thou heard'st me then, and gav'st him me;
Hear me again, I give him Thee.
He's mine, but more, O Lord, thine own,
For sure thy Grace on him is shown.
No freind I have like Thee to trust,
For mortall helpes are brittle Dust.
Preserve, O Lord, from stormes and wrack,
Protect him there, and bring him back;
And if thou shalt spare me a space,
That I again may see his face,
Then shall I celebrate thy Praise,
And Blesse Thee for't even all my Dayes.
If otherwise I goe to Rest,
Thy Will bee done, for that is best;
Perswade my heart I shall him see
For ever happefy'd with Thee.

ANNE BRADSTREET (1612–1672)

Occasional Meditations. From Charles E. Hambrick-Stowe, ed., *Early New England Meditative Poetry* (Mahwah, N.J.: Paulist Press, 1988), 84. The seventeenth-century spelling has been preserved in the two prayers by Anne Bradstreet, as in their copyrighted source.

In Thankfull Remembrance
for My Dear Husbands Safe Arrivall,
September 3, 1662

What shall I render to thy Name,
 Or how thy Praises speak;
My thankes how shall I testefye?
 O Lord, thou know'st I'm weak.
I owe so much, so little can
 Return unto thy Name,
Confusion seases on my Soul,
 And I am fill'd with shame.
O thou that hearest Prayers, Lord,
 To Thee shall come all Flesh;
Thou hast me heard and answered,
 My 'Plaints have had accesse.
What did I ask for but thou gav'st?
 What could I more desire?
But Thankfullness, even all my dayes,
 I humbly this Require.
Thy mercyes, Lord, have been so great,
 I number numberlies,
Impossible for to recount
 Or any way expresse.
O help thy Saints that sought thy Face,
 T' Return unto thee Praise,
And walk before thee as they ought,
 In strict and upright wayes.

ANNE BRADSTREET (1612–1672)
From Charles E. Hambrick-Stowe, ed., *Early New England Meditative Poetry* (Mahwah, N.J.: Paulist Press, 1988), 92.

For Heavenly Mindedness

O Thou Spirit of Life, breathe upon Thy graces in us, take us by the hand and lift us from earth, that we may see what glory Thou hast prepared for them that love Thee; through Jesus Christ our Lord. Amen.

RICHARD BAXTER (1615–1691)
From Selina F. Fox, *A Chain of Prayer across the Ages* (New York: E. P. Dutton & Co., 1963), 74.

The Invocation on the Lord's Day

O Eternal, Almighty, and most gracious God! heaven is thy throne, and earth is thy footstool; holy and reverend is thy name; thou art praised by the heavenly hosts, and in the congregation of thy saints on earth; and wilt be sanctified in all that come nigh unto thee. We are sinful and unworthy dust; but being invited by thee, are bold, through our blessed Mediator, to present ourselves and our supplications before thee. Receive us graciously, help us by thy Spirit; let thy fear be upon us; put thy laws into our hearts, and write them in our minds; let thy word come unto us in power, and be received in love, with attentive, reverent, and obedient minds. Make it to us the savour of life unto life. Cause us to be fervent in prayer, and joyful in thy praises, and to serve thee this day without distraction: that we may find that a day in thy courts is better than a thousand, and that it is good for us to draw near to God; through Jesus Christ our Lord and Saviour. Amen.

RICHARD BAXTER (1615–1691). From the Savoy Liturgy of 1660, designed for Nonconformist Protestant worship following the Restoration.
From C. W. Baird, *The Presbyterian Liturgies* (Grand Rapids: Baker Book House, 1959), 172–73.

Upon the Lord's Prayer

Our Father which in heaven art,
　　Thy name be always hallowed;
Thy kingdom come, thy will be done;
　　Thy heavenly path be followed:
By us on earth, as 'tis with thee,
　　We humbly pray;
And let our bread us given be
　　from day to day.
Forgive our debts, as we forgive
　　Those that to us indebted are;
Into temptation lead us not;
　　But save us from the wicked snare.
The kingdom's thine, the power too,
　　We thee adore;
The glory also shall be thine
　　For evermore.

JOHN BUNYAN (1628–1688)
From *Divine Emblems*, 447–48.

Teach Me Thy Ways

O God, guide of my youth, light of the blind, teacher of the ig-norant: thou enlightenest the simple, leadest wanderers back into the right path and drawest praise from the mouths of children.

Teach me thy ways and draw me away from the paths of the world. Tarry not, so that I may make haste; leave me no longer in the world and in sin.

O my Savior and my God, by pouring thy grace into my soul, make my heart desire Thee, and in desiring seek thee, and in seeking find thee, and in finding love thee. . . .

PIERRE JURIEU (1637–1713)
From Chapal and Pellegrin, *La tradition calvinienne*, 48. © Editions C.L.D. 1981. Used by permission.

In a Time of Torment

We have come to thee, O Lord, in times of trial and thou hast helped us. We have cried out of the depths and thou hast heard our voice. Who is like thee among the mighty, O God? Who like thee is magnificent in holiness, working wonders and worthy of reverent praise?

Continue thy benefits toward us throughout our pilgrimage and let us always understand that although thy children be surrounded by troubles on land and sea, thou dost nevertheless deliver them as thou pleasest.

Grant us more and more the grace to see in all thy past favors a firm argument for the continuation of thy bounty in the future, so that we may feel in our hearts the joy of those who turn toward thee and, trusting thy promises, may rest securely in thy goodness and place all our confidence and hope under the shadow of thy wings.

MONSIEUR DE RICHELIEU, Pastor. For the sailors of his congregation, 1659.
From Chapal and Pellegrin, *La tradition calvinienne*, 49. © Editions C.L.D. 1981. Used by permission.

Prayer for Zion

O Lord, our gracious God and Father, we offer thee our humble prayers asking that, if it please thee, thou wilt have mercy on thy poor and desolate Zion. She is afflicted, tempest-tossed, and destitute of all human consolation. She cries out in her distress: Alas, all you who pass by, look and see if there is any sorrow like my sorrow with which the Lord has afflicted me on the day of his fierce anger. She is at the summit of the rocks; in thy compassion gather her. Rekindle in this kingdom the flame of thy gospel which our sins have extinguished, and strengthen with invincible endurance those who want to revive it. Grant that neither death nor threats shall ever prevent them from preaching it until the last breath of their life, keeping safe from all dangers those who speak and those who hear. . . .

Thou wast willing to save Sodom and Gomorrah for the sake of ten righteous people; we offer thee thy Son who is worth more than all the righteous people who ever lived. For the sake of this righteous one, save us, Lord, for we perish.

CLAUDE BROUSSON (1647–1698). Prayer at the close of his sermon on the Mystic Dove. Found on persons arrested in the Vivarais region of south central France, 1701.
From Chapal and Pellegrin, *La tradition calvinienne*, 53. © Editions C.L.D. 1981. Used by permission.

General Prayer of Petition

And now, O most gracious God, Father and Fountain of mercy and goodness, who hast blessed us with the knowledge of our happiness and the way that leadeth unto it, excite in our souls such ardent desires after the one as may put us forth to the diligent prosecution of the other. Let us neither presume on our own strength, nor distrust thy divine assistance; but while we are doing our utmost endeavors, teach us still to depend on thee for success. Open our eyes, O God, and teach us out of thy law. Bless us with an exact and tender sense of our duty, and a knowledge to discern perverse things. Oh, that our ways were directed to keep thy statutes, then shall we not be ashamed when we have respect unto all thy commandments. Possess our hearts with a generous and holy disdain of all those poor enjoyments which this world holdeth out to allure us that they may never be able to inveigle our affections or betray us to any sin.Turn away our eyes from beholding vanity, and quicken thou us in thy law. Fill our souls with such a deep sense and full persuasion of those great truths which thou hast revealed in the gospel as may influence and regulate our whole conversation; and that the life which we henceforth live in the flesh, we may live through faith in the Son of God. Oh, that the infinite perfection of thy blessed nature, and the astonishing expressions of thy goodness and love, may conquer and overpower our hearts that they may be constantly rising towards thee in flames of the devoutest affection, and enlarging themselves in sincere and cordial love towards all the world, for thy sake; and that we may cleanse ourselves from all filthiness of flesh and spirit, perfecting holiness in thy fear, without which we can never hope to behold and enjoy thee. Finally, O God, grant that the consideration of what thou art, and what we ourselves are, may both humble and lay us low before thee and also stir up in us the strongest and most ardent aspirations towards thee! We desire to resign and give up ourselves to the conduct of thy Holy Spirit. Lead us in thy truth, and teach us, for thou art the God of our salvation. Guide us with thy counsel, and afterwards receive us unto glory, for the merits and intercession of thy blessed Son our Saviour. Amen.

HENRY SCOUGAL (1650–1678)
From *The Life of God in the Soul of Man* (Philadelphia: Westminster Press, 1948), 94–95.

Hymn of the Hungarian Galley Slaves

Lift up thy head, O Zion, weeping,
Still the Lord thy Father is;
Thou art daily in his keeping,
And thine every care is his.
Rise and be of gladsome heart,
And with courage play thy part;
Soon again his arms will fold thee
To his loving heart and hold thee.

Though the sea his waves assemble
And in fury fall on thee,
Though thou cry, with heart atremble,
"O my Savior, succor me!"
Though untroubled still he sleep
Who thy hope is on the deep,
Zion, calm the breast that quaketh;
Never God his own forsaketh.

Though the hills and vales be riven
God created with his hand,
Though the moving signs of heaven
Wars presage in every land,
Yet, O Zion, have no fear:
Ever is thy helper near;
He hath sought thee, he hath found thee;
Lo! His wings are walls around thee.

Though in chains thou now art grieving,
Though a tortured slave thou die,
Zion, if thou die believing,
Heaven's path shall open lie.
Upward gaze and happy be,
God hath not forsaken thee;
Thou his people art, and surely
He will fold his own securely. Amen.

KAROLY JESZENSKY (c. 1674)

Translated by William Toth. From United Church of Christ, *Pilgrim Hymnal* (1958), no. 377. Used by permission.

The Camisard Prayer

What are we, Lord, that thou art mindful of us? We who have changed thy grace into license and have run with the children of this world in the same dissolute abandon. Nevertheless, O Eternal One, despite all our excesses and profanities, thou hast remembered us in thy great compassion. The angel of thy Presence has gone before us. . . .

Continue then thy protection, O God, and cover us under the shadow of thy wings. Let thine angel of light go before us to lead us in the right path of truth. Scatter all the plots of our enemies; preserve us from their cruel designs; convert them to thyself. . . .

Grant us, O God, to will and to do according to thy good pleasure. Let not all the persecutions of our enemies turn us from the truth, but rather confirm us more and more in the path that leads to eternal bliss. Let neither death, nor life, nor things present, nor things to come ever separate us from the love thou hast shown toward us in thy dear Son, our Savior. . . .

ANONYMOUS CAMISARD (between 1685 and 1704). The Camisards were Protestants who withdrew to the mountains in southern France after the revocation of the Edict of Nantes (which had granted toleration) in 1685. Led by millennial prophets roused to ecstasy, some young Protestants assassinated a persecuting priest in 1702, sparking the Camisard wars. Perhaps named after their black peasant shirts, the Camisards organized and fought Louis XIV's soldiers fiercely but were effectively contained by 1704. Repudiated by a synod of the Reformed Church of France in 1715, they nevertheless remain an inspiration to many.

Royal archives of The Hague. From Chapal and Pellegrin, *La tradition calvinienne*, 55. © Editions C.L.D. 1981. Used by permission.

℘ The
Eighteenth Century

The eighteenth century was the era of the First Great Awakening in the American Colonies. Prayers offered during this revival were frequently not written down. It was, in fact, thought improper to use written prayers of any kind. Many believed that true prayer was of the heart and thus spontaneous. Thus, some of the significant persons of this century, such as Cotton Mather, Jonathan Edwards, and George Whitefield, are not included. No prayers by these giants can be found. The prayers that are included come from a variety of sources, among them poems in prayer form. These more formal styles of prayer were written and published. The authors in this century are either American or European.

The century begins with the prayers of Elizabeth Singer Rowe (1647–1737), a friend of Isaac Watts and a poet whose devotions were written during her lifetime but published only after her death. Bénédict Pictet (1655–1724), a Genevan by birth and pastor and professor of theology at the Academy there, was the author of several books. Matthew Henry (1662–1714), an English Nonconformist, was the author of one of the most important books on prayer, *A Method of Prayer*. Isaac Watts (1674–1748) could be called the father of the modern hymn because he liberated Reformed Christians from their slavery to the Psalter. In his paraphrases of the Psalms he included language about Jesus Christ and thus "Christianized" the Psalms. His hymns and paraphrases are to be found everywhere. Paul Raday (1677–1733), the first prominent lay leader of the Hungarian Reformed Church, was also a leader in the movement for Hungarian independence. Gerhard Tersteegen (1697–1769) was a German Pietist who is best known for his hymns. Philip Doddridge (1702–1751), an English Nonconformist who served as pastor of an Independent (Congregationalist) chapel, taught in an academy that prepared ministerial students. He wrote a great many hymns, as did Anne Steele (1716–1778), who was also English. Samuel Davies (1723–1761), an American Presbyterian pastor, served as president of the College of New Jersey (Princeton), succeeding Jonathan Edwards. Both of them died in office. John Witherspoon (1723–1794) was also a president of the College of New Jersey. He served as a member of the Continental Congress and was the only minister to sign the Declaration of Independence.

It is hard to characterize the prayers of this century. On the whole, they are more formal than those of the preceding century, probably because the less formal prayers were never written down. The piety they reflect was, in part, an effort to respond to Deism and rationalism by insisting on the central tenets of the Christian faith. It is important to note that most of the prayers that have been recorded from this century are either hymns or poems. All other forms of prayer were spontaneous and thus are lost to us.

A Prayer for Assurance of God's Presence

At thy command nature and necessity are no more; all things are alike easy to God. Speak but thou the word, and my desires are granted; say, "Let there be light," and there shall be light. Thou canst look me into peace, when the tumult of thoughts raise a storm within. Bid my soul be still, and all its tempests shall obey thee.

I depend upon thee; do thou smile and all the world may frown: do thou succeed my affairs, and I shall fear no obstacle that earth or hell can put in my way. Thou only art the object of my fear, and all my desires are directed to thee.

Let no appearance of created things, however specious, hide thee from my view; let me look through all to thee, nor cast a glance of love or hope below thee. With a holy contempt let me survey the ample round of the creation as lying in the hollow of thy hand, and every being in heaven and on earth as immoveable by the most potent cause in nature, till commissioned by thee to do good or hurt. O let thy hand be with me to keep me from evil, and let me abide under the shadow of the Almighty! I shall be secure in thy pavilion. To thee I fly for shelter from all the ills of mortality.

ELIZABETH SINGER ROWE (1647–1737)
From *Devout Exercises of the Heart*, 93–94.

A Devout Rapture

Thou radiant sun, thou moon, and all ye sparkling stars, how gladly would I leave your pleasant light to see the face of God! Ye crystal streams, ye groves and flowery lawns, my innocent delights, how joyfully could I leave you to meet that blissful prospect! and you, delightfulness of my friends, I would this moment quit you all to see him whom my soul loves; so loves, that I can find no words to express the unutterable ardor. Not as the miser loves his wealth, nor the ambitious his grandeur; not as the libertine loves his pleasure, or the generous man his friend; these are glad similitudes to describe such an intense passion as mine.

I love my friend; my vital breath and the light of heaven are dear to me; but should I say I love my God as I love these, I should belie the sacred flame which aspires to infinity. Tis thee, abstractly thee, O uncreated Beauty! that I love. In thee my wishes are all terminated; in thee, as in their blissful centre, all my desires meet, and there they must be eternally fixed; it is thou alone that must constitute my everlasting happiness.

ELIZABETH SINGER ROWE (1647–1737)
From *Devout Exercises of the Heart*, 145–46.

To the Holy Spirit

Holy Spirit, divine Consoler! Thou proceedest from the Father and the Son from all eternity. . . . Descend into our hearts today and make of them so many sanctuaries where Thou art pleased to dwell. Take from them all that might displease thee and be master there of all the faculties of our souls, all our passions, and all the members of our bodies. . . .

Teacher of truth, lead us into all truth; Holy Spirit, sanctify us; Spirit of life, enliven us; divine Consoler: console us in all our afflictions, sustain us in our struggles. . . .

Spirit of adoption, bear witness to our spirit that we are children of God, and make us cry Abba, Father. Spirit of glory, rest upon us until thou dost animate these ashes and resurrect our bodies to raise them to thine eternal dwelling place, where thou wilt be not only the seal of our redemption but the very basis of our joy. Amen.

BÉNÉDICT PICTET (1655–1724)
From Chapal and Pellegrin, *La tradition calvinienne*, 58. © Editions C.L.D. 1981. Used by permission.

For the Day Following a Fast

O Lord, hear the prayers that I have offered in thy house and pardon not only the sins I confessed to thee there but also those that were and are unrecognized, and the flaws in my devotion. In the name of thy dear Son, by his blood and by his obedience, I call upon thee. Out of love for him grant me grace; out of love for him send thy Spirit to convert me entirely, to transform me into thy image, and to make me able to fulfill all my promises and discharge my vows.

Hear also all the prayers offered to thee by thy church in general: for those who are under the cross; for the church of which I am a member by thy grace; for those who govern us, for those who teach us; for those who suffer in body, goods, or spirit; for all Thy children. O God, be swayed by our supplications and convert us all. Amen.

BÉNÉDICT PICTET (1655–1724)
From Chapal and Pellegrin, *La tradition calvinienne*, 59. © Editions C.L.D. 1981. Used by permission.

A Morning Prayer

O Lord, lift up the light of Thy countenance upon us; let Thy peace rule in our hearts, and may it be our strength and our song, in the house of our pilgrimage. We commit ourselves to Thy care and keeping this day; let Thy grace be mighty in us, and sufficient for us, and let it work in us both to will and to do of Thine own good pleasure, and grant us strength for all the duties of the day. Keep us from sin. Give us the rule over our own spirits and keep us from speaking unadvisedly with our lips. May we live together in peace and holy love, and do Thou command Thy blessing upon us, even life for evermore. Prepare us for all the events of the day; for we know not what a day may bring forth. Give us grace to deny ourselves; to take up our cross daily, and to follow in the steps of our Lord and Master, Jesus Christ our Lord. Amen.

MATTHEW HENRY (1662–1714)
From Selina F. Fox, *A Chain of Prayer across the Ages* (New York: E. P. Dutton & Co., 1943), 45.

Prayer of Praise

My God, how endless is Thy love!
Thy gifts are every evening new;
And morning mercies from above
Gently distill like early dew.

Thou spread'st the curtains of the night,
Great Guardian of my sleeping hours;
Thy sovereign word restores the light,
And quickens all my waking powers.

I yield my powers to Thy command,
To Thee I consecrate my days;
Perpetual blessings from Thy hand
Demand perpetual songs of praise.

ISAAC WATTS (1674–1748)
From Presbyterian Church in the U.S.A., *The Hymnal* (1933), no. 78.

A Prayer of Confidence
(Paraphrase of Psalm 23)

My shepherd will supply my need;
Jehovah is His name:
In pastures fresh He makes me feed,
Beside the living stream.
He brings my wandering spirit back,
When I forsake His ways;
And leads me, for his mercy's sake,
In paths of truth and grace.

When I walk through the shades of death
Your presence is my stay;
One word of Your supporting breath
Drives all my fears away.
Your hand, in sight of all my foes,
Does still my table spread;
My cup with blessings overflows,
Your oil anoints my head.

The sure provisions of my God
Attend me all my days;
O may Your house be my abode,
And all my work be praise.
There would I find a settled rest,
While others go and come;
No more a stranger, or a guest,
But like a child at home.

ISAAC WATTS (1674–1748)

From Presbyterian Church (U.S.A.), *The Presbyterian Hymnal* (1990), no. 172.

A Prayer for the Lord's Day

Eternal and most glorious God,
you dwell in light which no one can approach,
and live and reign for ever and ever:
we bless you that you have brought us by your grace
to see the light of another day.
Help us, O Lord, this day
to commemorate the rising of our blessed Redeemer;
and let our hearts be raised to the heavenly world,
and to Jesus, who sits at your right hand in glory.
May the blessed Holy Spirit visit us with divine influence,
and remain with us in both public and private worship,
for without the blessed Spirit's gracious assistance,
we can do nothing that is acceptable to you.

May we attend with cheerfulness and holy desire
on the ordinances of your house this day,
and may we find your presence in the assembly of your people.
May our souls be lifted up to you
in the prayers that will be offered,
and may our lips sing your praises with holy joy.
Let us come away from your house
under the light of your countenance,
satisfied with your love
declared to the world in Christ Jesus our Lord. Amen.

ISAAC WATTS (1674–1748)
From Uniting Church in Australia, *Uniting in Worship*, 226–27.

Prayer of Adoration

I adore Thee and glorify thee, O everlastingly worshiped Holy Trinity, complete and One God Almighty. Veneration and honor unto thee from all living creatures.

Glory to the Father, who created me. Glory to the Son, who redeemed me, Glory to the Holy Spirit, who sanctified me.

Glory to God, the Father, who preserves me by his power. Glory to God, the Son, who guides me by his grace. Glory to God, the Holy Spirit, who sanctifies me through his love. Let the whole and undivided Holy Trinity be forever hallowed! Let the sacred name of the Holy Trinity be forever adored by all angels above and all living creatures here below, now and forever. Amen.

PAUL RADAY (1677–1733). Raday was one of the greatest lay church leaders of his time in Hungary. The Raday Kollegium, a faculty of the Hungarian Reformed University on Raday Street in Budapest, was named for him.
English translation by Stephen Szabo. Used by permission.

Prayer of a Day Laborer

O God! I am receiving my daily bread by the hard work of my two hands, with which I earn my bread daily and my attire. From early dawn till late sunset day after day the burden of my work causes me to languish and the extreme heat of the sun fatigues me. I have no other way than this much daily labor to sustain my life and the life of my own household: unceasing labor day after day, and the hope that after each night's short sleep I will be able to work next day until night again.

In spite of all, I would not think of grumbling. Instead, with sincere thanksgiving I praise Thy Holy Name for keeping me in good health and vigor till this very day, providing graciously for my daily needs. To rise so early every morning and to go to bed so exhausted every night while earning my daily bread with so much sweat would be in vain, if Thou didst not send Thy blessings on me, O Lord!

Do not let me stand in idleness, my God; call me and send me to join all Thy hard workers in the vineyard. Do not let me serve Thee carelessly and never let me become a burden to others. Then when the last night of my earthly life will come, give me the good reward I deserve for all my laborious work on earth. Amen.

ANONYMOUS HUNGARIAN PROTESTANT (1746)
English translation by Stephen Szabo. Used by permission.

For Surrender to God's Service

Let Thy love so warm our souls, O Lord, that we may gladly surrender ourselves with all we are and have unto Thee. Let Thy love fall as fire from heaven upon the altar of our hearts; teach us to guard it heedfully by continual devotion and quietness of mind, and to cherish with anxious care every spark of its holy flame, with which Thy good Spirit would quicken us, so that neither height, nor depth, things present, nor things to come, may ever separate us therefrom. Strengthen Thou our wills, animate our cold hearts with Thy warmth and tenderness that we may no more live as in a dream, but walk before Thee as pilgrims in earnest to reach their home. And grant us all at last to meet with Thy holy saints before Thy throne, and there rejoice in Thy love. Amen.

GERHARD TERSTEEGEN (1697–1769)
From Selina F. Fox, *A Chain of Prayer across the Ages* (New York: E. P. Dutton & Co., 1943), 99.

A Morning Supplication

O Great and lofty God, Thou Father in the Highest, Who hast promised to dwell with them that are of a lowly spirit and fear Thy Word; create now in us such lowly hearts, and give us a reverential awe of Thy commandments. O come, Thou Spirit of Strength, and arouse our souls to hunger and thirst after Thee, their true Guide, that they may be sustained by Thine all powerful influence. Arise, O Spirit of Life, that through Thee we may begin to live; descend upon us and transform us into such human beings as the heart of God longs to see, renewed into the image of Christ, and going on from glory to glory. O God, Thou Supreme Good, make Thyself known to us; through Jesus Christ our Lord. Amen.

GERHARD TERSTEEGEN (1697–1769)
From Selina F. Fox, *A Chain of Prayer across the Ages* (New York: E. P. Dutton & Co., 1943), 141.

For a Constant Sense
of God's Presence

O God our heavenly Father, renew in us the sense of Thy gracious Presence, and let it be a constant impulse within us to peace, trustfulness, and courage on our pilgrimage. Let us hold Thee fast with a loving and adoring heart, and let our affections be fixed on Thee, that so the unbroken communion of our hearts with Thee may accompany us whatsoever we do, through life and in death. Teach us to pray heartily; to listen for Thy voice within, and never to stifle its warnings. Behold, we bring our poor hearts as a sacrifice unto Thee; come and fill Thy sanctuary, and suffer nought impure to enter there. O Thou who art Love, let Thy Divine Spirit flow like a river through our whole souls, and lead us in the right way till we pass into the Land of Promise; through Jesus Christ. Amen.

GERHARD TERSTEEGEN (1697–1769)
From Selina F. Fox, *A Chain of Prayer across the Ages* (New York: E. P. Dutton & Co., 1943), 147.

Prayer for Approach
to the Lord's Table

Blessed Lord, I adore Thy wise and gracious appointments for the edification of Thy church in holiness and in love. I thank Thee that thou hast commanded thy servants to form themselves into societies; and I adore my gracious Saviour who has instituted, as with his dying breath, the holy solemnity of his supper, to be through all ages a memorial of his dying love, and a bond of that union which it is his sovereign pleasure that his people should preserve. I hope thou, Lord, art witness to the sincerity with which I desire to give myself up to thee; and that I may call thee to record on my soul; that if I now hesitate about this particular manner of doing it, it is not because I would allow myself to break any of thy commands, or to slight any of thy favours. I trust, thou knowest that my present delay arises only from an uncertainty as to my own duty, and a fear of profaning holy things by an unworthy approach to them. Yet, surely, O Lord, if thou hast given me a reverence for thy command, a desire of communion with thee, and a willingness to devote myself wholly to thy service, I may regard it as a token for good that thou art disposed to receive me, and that I am not wholly unqualified for an ordinance which I so highly honor, and so earnestly desire; I therefore make mine humble request unto thee, O Lord, this day, that thou wouldst graciously be pleased to instruct me in my duty, and to teach me the way which I should take! Examine me, O Lord, and prove me, try my reins and my heart. Is there any secret sin, in the love and practice of which I would indulge? Is there any of the precepts in the habitual breach of which I would allow myself? Let me not, then, wrong mine own soul by a causeless and sinful absence from thy sacred table. Scatter my remaining doubts, if thou seest they have no just foundation. Fill me with a more assured faith, with a more ardent love; and plead thine own cause with my heart in such a manner as that I may not be able any longer to delay that approach. And I earnestly pray, that all who profess to have received Christ Jesus the Lord may be duly careful to walk with him, and that we may be all preparing for the general assembly of the first-born, and may join in that nobler and more immediate worship, where all these types and shadows shall be laid aside; where even these memorials shall be no longer necessary, but a living present Redeemer shall be the everlasting joy of those who in his absence have delighted to commemorate his death. Amen.

PHILIP DODDRIDGE (1702–1751)
From *The Rise and Progress of Religion in the Soul*, 182–84. Philadelphia: Presbyterian Board of Christian Education, n.d.

Father of Mercies

Father of mercies, in Thy Word what endless glory shines;
Forever be Thy Name adored for these celestial lines.

Here the Redeemer's welcome voice spreads heavenly
    peace around;
And life and everlasting joys attend the blissful sound.

O may these heavenly pages be my ever dear delight;
And still new beauties may I see, and still increasing light.

Divine Instructor, gracious Lord, be Thou forever near;
Teach me to love Thy sacred Word, and view my Saviour there.

ANNE STEELE (1716–1778)
From Presbyterian Church in the U.S.A., *The Hymnal* (1933), no. 218.

Lord, I Am Thine

Lord, I am Thine, entirely Thine,
Purchased and saved by blood divine.
With full consent Thine I would be,
And own Thy sov'reign right in me.

Grant one poor sinner more a place
Among the children of Thy grace;
A wretched sinner lost to God,
But ransomed by Immanuel's blood.

Thine would I live, Thine would I die,
Be Thine through all eternity;
The vow is passed beyond repeal;
Now will I set the solemn seal.

Here at the cross where flows the blood
That bought my guilty soul for God;
Thee, my new Master, now I call,
And consecrate to Thee my all.

Do Thou assist a feeble worm
The great engagement to perform;
Thy grace can full assistance lend,
And on that grace I dare depend.

SAMUEL DAVIES (1723–1761)
From Presbyterian Church in the U.S., *New Psalms and Hymns* (1901), no. 318.

Prayer for the Nation

God grant that in America true religion and civil liberty may be inseparable, and that the unjust attempts to destroy the one, may in the issue tend to [the] support and establishment of both.

JOHN WITHERSPOON (1723–1794). The end of a sermon preached at Princeton, New Jersey, May 1776.

From Louis B. Weeks, "John Witherspoon, Presbyterian Revolutionary," *The Presbyterian Survey*, September 1975, p. 6.

☞ The
Nineteenth Century

The nineteenth century is represented by more American prayers than any previous century. This is the century that also witnessed the beginnings of the social gospel and the explicit concern for justice. The Industrial Revolution in Europe and America had displaced rural people and created urban slums; people were inadequately housed, poorly fed, and laboring in terrible conditions. In this setting, it was proper that Christian prayers take into account the lives of those who were at the bottom of the economic ladder as well as those who oppressed them. Slavery was also an issue of great importance, although the prayers do not, as a whole, reflect that concern. Some of the authors included in this century were involved in the abolition movement, and at least one (Francis Grimké) had been a slave. In the United States, a wave of revival swept the churches both at the beginning of the century (the Second Great Awakening) and at the end of the century (the missionary revival). This later revival produced a wave of idealistic missionaries who spread Christianity to all parts of the world through an aggressive movement to win the "world for Christ in our generation." The prayers in this volume are, however, limited to Europe and America because converts in the nations to which the gospel was taken had not yet become leaders in the churches and their prayers are not recorded.

Timothy Dwight (1752–1817), grandson of Jonathan Edwards, was the president of Yale College whose preaching resulted in the conversion of one-third of the students in 1802. This was the real beginning of the Second Great Awakening. He was an influential Congregational minister of modified Calvinist leanings. Friedrich Schleiermacher (1768–1834) was a German Reformed pastor, theologian, and biblical scholar whose concern to make faith intelligible in the modern world led to a strong emphasis on human experience. He has been called the father of modern theology and the reviver of Reformed consciousness in the modern era. Thomas Chalmers (1780–1847) was an eminent Scottish churchman and theologian who led in the creation of the Free Church of Scotland. Ferenc Kölesey (1790–1838) was a Hungarian poet, philosopher, and patriot who shared in Hungary's struggle for independence from Austria. His prayer became the national anthem of that new nation in 1848. Poet and pastor Henry Francis Lyte (1793–1847) was a Scot whose contributions to hymnody are significant. Charles Hodge (1797–1878), longtime professor at Princeton, was a spokesperson for the Old School among Presbyterians and a theologian who helped to preserve orthodox Calvinism.

Félix Neff (1798–1829), a Genevan whose conversion was strongly influenced by the Moravians, served as an evangelist in Switzerland and France before being ordained in London. Albert Barnes (1798–1870) was a pastor, social reformer, and leader in the New School branch of American Presbyterianism. Adolphe Monod (1802–1856) was a French pastor whose sermons drew large audiences. H. F. Kohlbrugge (1803–1875), pastor of a Reformed Church in Germany, was an independent Calvinist whose influence on major theologians stretched into the twentieth century. Napoléon Roussel (1805–1878) was a French Reformed pastor with Methodist leanings. Caroline Malvesin (1806–1889) was the founder of a community of deaconesses. Madame André Walther (1807–1886) was a Pietist of high social rank in Paris and an early leader of French Protestant feminism. Horatius Bonar (1808–1889) was a Scottish pastor best known for his hymns.

Three writers of prayers stand out as having tremendous influence on the social fabric of America. Ann Plato (dates unknown) was a teacher in the "colored" school associated with the predominantly black Fifth Congregational Church in Hartford, Connecticut. Harriet Beecher Stowe (1811–1896), daughter of the famous Lyman Beecher and sister of Henry Ward Beecher, was best known for her influential book *Uncle Tom's Cabin*, which had a profound impact, increasing antislavery feelings in America. Henry Ward Beecher (1813–1887) was probably the single most influential preacher in America during the last half of the nineteenth century.

George MacDonald (1824–1905) was a Scottish preacher and novelist who spoke in language that ordinary people could understand. He was very popular in his time and lives on in his fictional work, which is still widely read. He has been called the Reformed C. S. Lewis. Madame Henri Mirabaud (1827–1893), a French Protestant, is known for her book of prayers for families. J. H. Gunning (1829–1905) was a Dutch pastor and theologian whose evangelical leanings moderated his Calvinism. Emily Dickinson (1830–1886), an American poet who was raised in a strict Calvinist home, became a recluse and is known through her poetry. Alexander Whyte (1836–1921) was the greatest preacher in Scotland in the late nineteenth and early twentieth centuries. A leading evangelical, he welcomed the new science of biblical criticism. Dwight Lyman Moody (1837–1899), the American evangelist, was the first to develop a form of evangelism specifically designed for urban people. Jan Karafiát (1846–1929) was a Czech Reformed minister and Bible translator especially remembered for his children's story "The Fireflies." Francis A. Grimké (1850–1937) was a leading African American preacher and church leader among American Presbyterians. Benjamin B. Warfield (1851–1921) was the major proponent of Princeton theology. After a period as professor at Western Theological Seminary, he succeeded A. A. Hodge in the chair of didactic and polemical theology at Princeton and taught there until his death. Charles Spurgeon (1834–1892), was an influential preacher in England who, though a Baptist, was a thoroughgoing Calvinist.

From our point of view, many nineteenth-century prayers are overly long and wordy. They were written to express the point of view of the author. Many of the authors represented here were concerned about theology, either to protect or to modify classical Calvinism. Since the prayers were written to be published, the authors aimed to express themselves carefully and accurately. Many of the poems and prayer hymns, however, are warm and personal. In these the passion of the heart is poured out.

I Love Thy Kingdom, Lord

I love Thy Kingdom, Lord,
The house of Thine abode,
The church our blest Redeemer saved
With His own precious blood.

I love Thy church, O God:
Her walls before Thee stand.
Dear as the apple of Thine eye,
And graven on Thy hand.

For her my tears shall fall,
For her my prayers ascend;
To her my cares and toils be given,
Till toils and cares shall end.

Beyond my highest joy,
I prize her heavenly ways,
Her sweet communion, solemn vows,
Her hymns of love and praise.

Sure as Thy truth shall last,
To Zion shall be given
The brightest glories earth can yield,
And brighter bliss of heaven.

TIMOTHY DWIGHT (1752–1817)
From Presbyterian Church in the U.S.A., *The Hymnal* (1933), no. 337.

In a Time of Bereavement

Holy and merciful God and Father! We adore in deep humility your inscrutable wisdom, which has numbered and ordained the days of each person's life. And even though, before the days run out, one person may have come closer to the common goal of our destiny than another, we entrust to you with childlike confidence all those whom you have called away from this earthly theater. We firmly believe that you, who gave your Son all authority in heaven and on earth, also know how to take care that he lose nothing you have given to him; for none of your eternal and blessed decrees can go unfulfilled. Yes, through him and for his sake you will lead all to salvation, because we know that you sent your Son into the world not to judge the world, but to save it. But grant to us who are still pilgrims on this earth an ever richer enjoyment of eternal life in conformity to him whom you have loved, and in whom you love us. May our pain and sorrow, as well as our joy and peace, contribute to the strengthening of this life in us; and may it obtain for us the power through which we overcome death itself and the fear of death. Amen.

FRIEDRICH D. E. SCHLEIERMACHER (1768–1834)

From *Servant of the Word: Selected Sermons of Friedrich Schleiermacher*, 208. Translated with an introduction by Dawn DeVries. Copyright 1987 by Fortress Press. Used by permission of Augsburg Fortress.

A Prayer for Peace

So teach us to number our days that we may apply our hearts to wisdom. Lighten, if it be your will, the pressure of this world's care, and, above all, reconcile us to your will, and give us a peace which the world cannot take away; through Jesus Christ our Lord. Amen.

THOMAS CHALMERS (1780–1847)
From Selina F. Fox, *A Chain of Prayer across the Ages* (New York: E. P. Dutton & Co., 1943), 116.

Hungarian National Hymn

God bless all Hungarians
with good cheer in full measure!
Defend them with thy mighty arm
When they face the oppressor.
Torn by fate for a span of time,
Give now glad future years!
They have suffered long enough
For time past and to come.

FERENC KÖLESEY (1790–1838)
Translated by Stephen Szabo. Used by permission.

Commitment to Christ

Jesus, I my cross have taken
All to leave and follow Thee;
Destitute, despised, forsaken,
Thou from hence my all shalt be.
Perish every fond ambition,
All I've sought or hoped or known;
Yet how rich is my condition;
God and heaven are still my own.

Man may trouble and distress me,
'Twill but drive me to Thy breast;
Life with trials hard may press me,
Heaven will bring me sweeter rest;
O 'tis not in grief to harm me
While Thy love is left to me,
O 'twere not in joy to charm me,
Were that joy unmixed with Thee.

Take, my soul, thy full salvation.
Rise o'er sin and fear and care;
Joy to find in every station,
Something still to do or bear;
Think what Spirit dwells within thee,
What a Father's smile is thine.
What a Saviour died to win thee;
Child of heaven, shouldst thou repine?

HENRY FRANCIS LYTE (1793–1847)
From Presbyterian Church in the U.S.A., *The Hymnal* (1933), no. 274.

Come, Holy Spirit

Come, Holy Spirit, come! Descend in all Thy plenitude of grace. Come as the Spirit of reverence and love. Aid us, O God, in the discharge of the duties on which we are about to enter. We have assembled here from almost all parts of the world. We have come to confess Thee before men; to avow our faith that Thou art, and that Thou art the Creator, Preserver and Governor of the World. We are here to acknowledge that the God of Abraham, and of Isaac, and of Jacob is our God. We are here to confess Christ as God manifest in the flesh, and as our only and all-sufficient Saviour, who for us sinners died upon the cross to reconcile us unto God and has risen again in victory over the grave. We acknowledge that all power in heaven and on earth is committed to his hands. Thanks be to God, thanks be to God, that He has put on us, unworthy as we are, the honor to make this confession, and to bear this testimony. O God, look down from heaven upon us. Shed abroad in our hearts the Holy Spirit, that we may be truly one in Christ Jesus.

O Thou blessed Spirit of the living God, without whom the universe were dead, Thou art the source of all life, of all holiness, of all power. Come, we pray, and dwell in every heart, and touch every lip. Bless this Evangelical Alliance as we spread abroad our banner in the sight of all with the confession which Thou hast put into our lips—the confession of all Christendom. We confess God the Father to be our Father; Jesus Christ, His Son, to be our Saviour; the Holy Ghost to be our Sanctifier; and His Word to be the infallible rule of faith and practice. Grant, O Lord, that wherever human words are uttered, this confession may be the language of every heart. And to the Father, Son, and Holy Ghost be glory, now and evermore. Amen.

CHARLES HODGE (1797–1878). This prayer was offered at the opening of the Sixth General Conference of the Evangelical Alliance in New York City in the summer of 1874.
From Evangelical Alliance, *The History, Essays, Orations and Other Addresses of the Sixth General Conference of the Evangelical Alliance*, 11–12. Adapted by William O. Harris.

When, Then, Will We Be Wise?

O God, to what illusions we poor humans are subject! When, then, will we be wise? O, when wilt thou no longer need to make us fail at every step in order to break this miserable pride? O, when will this hydra be destroyed and these poisoned heads quit growing back? O Lord, be faithful to bring us down in the measure that we vaunt ourselves. Do not spare us humiliations: make us understand that the old man must die and that opprobrium, bitterness, and hate are the only foods that do not sustain him. O, give us this gall to drink, so bitter to our palate and yet, afterward, so sweet to our heart! Remove this corrupted flesh despite our cries, and do not spare us the punishment so necessary for us. Only grant us to seek thee always, without ceasing, in the form of thy suffering, so that we may find and possess thee forever! Amen.

FÉLIX NEFF (1798–1829)
From Chapal and Pellegrin, *La tradition calvinienne*, 61. © Editions C.L.D. 1981. Used by permission.

Pastoral Prayer

O Thou, who hast characterized thyself as the hearer of prayer, unto thee shall all flesh come: and that we may come with acceptance and success, we come in the name of the great intercessor, Jesus Christ, the righteous—and thou Eternal Spirit of grace and supplication, do thou make intercession for us, by making intercession in us, according to the will of God.

Bless the services in which we were engaged on the past day. Let a savour of divine things be left on our spirits, and be diffused in our conversation. Let those around us take knowledge of us, that we have been with Jesus; and may our profiting appear unto all men. May our light shine before men. May we be manifestly the disciples of Christ. May we put on, as the elect of God, holy and beloved, bowels of mercies, kindness, humbleness of mind, meekness, long suffering, forgiving one another. May we be followers of God, as dear children; may we be perfect, as our Father, who is in heaven, is perfect.

We confess and bewail, not only our deficiencies, but our backslidings also. O, recall us to thyself; enable us to feel our first love, and to do our first works. Yea, may we forget the things that are behind, and reach forth unto those that are before. May we not only have life, but may we have it more abundantly; and not only be fruitful, but bear much fruit. . . .

May the dead hear the voice of the Son of God, and live. May those who are asking the way to Zion, with their faces thitherward, find a teacher that will say to them, This is the way, walk ye in it, when they turn to the right hand, and when they turn to the left. Let the rich be poor in spirit; and the poor be made rich in faith, and heirs of the kingdom which thou hast promised to them that love thee. Let the ignorant be enlightened; and let those that are wise, become fools, that they may be wise. . . .

ALBERT BARNES (1798–1870)
From *Prayers for the Use of Families* (1850), 57–58.

Direct Us

God of Jeremiah! God of Jesus Christ! We know that "it is not within man that walketh to direct his steps," and we come to thee to place in thy fatherly hands the direction of our path. "Punish us, but within measure, and not in thine anger, lest thou utterly destroy us." Let lightning split the clouds to disclose to us, through our darkness, thy plan and thy designs, into which we henceforth wish to enter without reservations.

Put an end to our infinite perplexities, our perpetual stumblings, our unprincipled society, our church without community, our Christianity without the Christian life!

Furthermore, Lord, speak instead of the one who is speaking. . . . It is thee alone whom he awaits to guide this people and to guide him in the paths where thou deignest to be found.

ADOLPHE MONOD (1802–1856). The quotations are from Jeremiah 10:23–24, King James
    Version, adapted to reflect more closely the Segond Version used by Monod.
From Chapal and Pellegrin, *La tradition calvinienne*, 62. © Editions C.L.D. 1981. Used by permission.

Prayer before the Sermon

Lord Jesus Christ, gracious and merciful God! We thank thee for thy grace, that thou hast brought us together in this morning hour on thy day, to hear the apostolic word. We pray that, through the grace of thy Holy Spirit, we will receive thy Word in our hearts as a Word that concerns *us*, that it not be preached to us as though we had deaf ears—rather, that we take thy truth to heart, because there is nothing more salutary for us than to be humbled by thy hand, so that it is thou alone who makest us great. . . .

O Lord God, we confess before thee our terrible trespasses and great sins. O, who are we that thou shouldst think of us and visit us with thy Word? There is nothing in us but wrong, sin, and rebellion against thy holy will. Deal with us according to thy great mercy, that we not deceive ourselves and travel the path to hell.

Almighty God, make us alive with thy Word, and draw us to thee, through the power of thy grace. Thou knowest in what wretchedness we find ourselves and how terrible life appears to us, in whom lives nothing but sin, the devil, and the world—the powers that would rob us of our crown. Remember us according to thy mercy, now that we come to thee to be made whole in faith, to leave the unholy way and be brought into the right way.

Come, bend our wills so that we shall be content with thy will. Make us truly humble before thee. Let our eyes be focused on Jesus Christ, that we may seek in him our salvation and our righteousness. Be a husband to widows, a father to orphans, and a comforter to the grieving! All that thou doest, thou doest to draw us to thee. Remember this city, the entire country, our king and his government, and let thy Word run its course. Gracious God, remember us according to thy mercy, so that we may bow before thy Word, and that we may be happy under thy correction, under thy Word, under thy peace. Amen.

H. F. KOHLBRUGGE (1803–1875)

From *Gebeden uitgesproken bij de openbare godsdienstoeferningen* (Prayers offered in public worship) (Amsterdam, 1950), 60–61. Translated by Stanley W. Bamberg and James E. Davison.

Our Empty Words

What a frightful account we will have to give to thee, O God, to thee who judgest and condemnest the words we speak! If vain words will be condemned, what then of malicious, venomous words? And if our words merit such severe judgment, what will our deeds merit? O Lord, Lord, do not settle accounts with us! Pardon us first: then change us and in the future let no words cross our lips save those inspired by this thought, that thy Son, so full of love, was called the Word.

NAPOLÉON ROUSSEL (1805–1878)

From Chapal and Pellegrin, *La tradition calvinienne*, 63. © Editions C.L.D. 1981. Used by permission.

Here I Am

Blessed art thou, O Lord;
Here I am to do thy will!
Here I am, through with the world;
Thou hast said to me:
   "In returning and rest shall ye be saved;
   in quietness and in confidence shall be your strength."
How faithful thou art! As soon as it seemed good to thee, thou hadst
      pity on me,
thou heardest me. Thou preparest a way before my feet and sayest:
   "This is the way, walk ye in it," without turning either to the right
   or to the left.
Yes, here I am to do thy will!
Let me no longer belong to myself, but to thee . . . all to thee . . .
   and then thou wilt be all to me. . . .
Thou seemest to make me know that, because of thy blessings,
I have nothing more to fear from the world, nor from the hardness of
      my heart,
which long kept me from the refreshing spring to which thou didst
      invite me
   during so many years.
I pray thee, Lord, to increase my faith and my fervor in prayer.
Hasten the moment of revelation of thy grace for many souls, for
      all souls!
Amen.

SISTER CAROLINE MALVESIN (1806–1889). The quotations are from Isaiah 30:15 and 21,
   King James Version.
From Chapal and Pellegrin, *La tradition calvinienne*, 66. © Editions C.L.D. 1981. Used by permission.

I Pass by Indifferent

Jesus, Just and Holy One . . . , thou liftest up the weak and weepest with those who weep; thou didst take part in the simple joys of the wedding at Cana! And I? My eyes always turned toward heaven, I often pass by indifferent to those who cry out for my sympathy, and my lack of charitable love can make others accuse thy doctrine of drying up the heart. O thou who allowest me to count myself among thy disciples, change these bad attitudes that remain in my heart. Amen.

MADAME ANDRÉ WALTHER (1807–1886)
From Chapal and Pellegrin, *La tradition calvinienne*, 64. © Editions C.L.D. 1981. Used by permission.

Prayer for God's Presence

Come, Lord, and tarry not;
Bring the long-looked-for day;
O why these years of waiting here,
These ages of delay?

Come, for Thy saints still wait;
Daily ascends their sigh;
The Spirit and the Bride say, "Come."
Dost Thou not hear the cry?

Come, for creation groans,
Impatient of Thy stay,
Worn out with these long years of ill,
These ages of delay.

Come and make all things new;
Build up this ruined earth;
Restore our faded Paradise,
Creation's second birth.

Come, and begin Thy reign
Of everlasting peace;
Come, take the Kingdom to Thyself,
Great King of Righteousness.

HORATIUS BONAR (1808–1889)
From Presbyterian Church in the U.S.A., *The Hymnal* (1933), no. 188.

Prayer for Sacramental Presence

Here, O my Lord, I see Thee face to face;
Here would I touch and handle things unseen,
Here grasp with firmer hand eternal grace,
And all my weariness upon Thee lean.

Here would I feed upon the bread of God,
Here drink with Thee the royal wine of heaven;
Here would I lay aside each earthly load,
Here taste afresh the calm of sin forgiven.

This is the hour of banquet and of song;
This is the heavenly table spread for me:
Here let me feast, and, feasting, still prolong
The brief, bright hour of fellowship with Thee.

I have no help but Thine, nor do I need
Another arm save Thine to lean upon:
It is enough, my Lord, enough indeed;
My strength is in Thy might, Thy might alone.

HORATIUS BONAR (1808–1889)
From Presbyterian Church in the U.S.A., *The Hymnal* (1933), no. 352.

A Teacher's Prayer

Teach me, O Lord, the secret errors of my way,
Teach me the paths wherein I go astray,
Learn me the way to teach the word of love,
For that's the pure intelligence above.
As well as learning, give me that truth forever—
What a mere worldly tie can never sever,
For though our bodies die, our souls will live forever,
To cultivate in every youthful mind,
Habitual grace, and sentiments refined.
Thus while I strive to govern the human heart,
May I the heavenly precepts still impart;
Oh! May each youthful bosom catch the sacred fire,
And youthful mind to virtue's throne aspire.
Now fifteen years their destined course have run,
In fast succession round the central sun;
How did the follies of that period pass,
I ask myself—are they inscribed in brass?
Oh! Recollection, speed their fresh return,
And sure 'tis mine to be ashamed and mourn
"What shall I ask, or what refrain to say?
Where shall I point, or how conclude my lay?"
So much my weakness needs—so oft thy voice
Assures that weakness, and confirms my choice.
Oh, grant me active days of peace and truth,
Strength to my heart, and wisdom to my youth,
A sphere of usefulness—a soul to fill
That sphere with duty, and perform thy will.

ANN PLATO (fl. 1841)

From J. M. Washington, *Conversations with God: Two Centuries of Prayers by African Americans* (New York: HarperCollins, 1994), 38.

Delight in God's Presence

Still, still with Thee, when purple morning breaketh,
When the bird waketh, and the shadows flee;
Fairer than morning, lovelier than daylight,
Dawns the sweet consciousness, I am with Thee.

Alone with Thee, amid the mystic shadows,
The solemn hush of nature newly born;
Alone with Thee in breathless adoration,
In the calm dew and freshness of the morn.

Still, still with Thee! As to each new-born morning
A fresh and solemn splendor still is given,
So does this blessed consciousness awaking,
Breathe each day nearness unto Thee and heaven.

So shall it be at last, in that bright morning,
When the soul waketh and life's shadows flee;
O in that hour, fairer than daylight dawning
Shall rise the glorious thought, I am with Thee.

HARRIET BEECHER STOWE (1811–1896)
From Presbyterian Church in the U.S.A., *The Hymnal* (1933), no. 107.

Unanswered Prayer

Thou hast called us to Thyself, most merciful Father, with love and with promises abundant; and we are witnesses that it is not in vain that we drew near to Thee. We bear witness to Thy faithfulness. Thy promises are Yea and Amen. Thy blessings are exceeding abundant, more than we know or think. We thank Thee for the privilege of prayer, and for Thine answers to prayer; and we rejoice that Thou dost not answer according to our petitions. We are blind, and are constantly seeking things which are not best for us. If Thou didst grant all our desires according to our requests, we should be ruined. In dealing with our little children we give them, not the things which they ask for, but the things which we judge to be best for them; and Thou, our Father, art by Thy providence overruling our ignorance and our headlong mistakes, and art doing for us, not so much the things that we request of Thee as the things that we should ask; and we are, day by day, saved from peril and from ruin by Thy better knowledge and by Thy careful love. Amen.

HENRY WARD BEECHER (1813–1887)
From H. E. Fosdick, *The Meaning of Prayer* (New York: Follett Publishing Co., 1949), 111.

Acceptance of God's Will

I said, "Let me walk in the fields."
　　He said, "Nay, walk in the town."
I said, "There are no flowers there."
　　He said, "No flowers, but a crown."

I said, "But the sky is black,
　　There is nothing but noise and din."
But he wept as he sent me back—
　　"There is more," he said, "there is sin."

GEORGE MACDONALD (1824–1905)
From Horton Davies, ed., *The Communion of Saints: Prayers of the Famous* (Grand Rapids: Wm. B. Eerdmans
　　Publishing Co., 1949), 101.

Prayer

My prayers, my God, flow from what I am not;
I think thy answers make me what I am.
Like weary waves thought follows upon thought,
But the still depth beneath is all thine own,
And there thou mov'st in paths to us unknown.
Out of strange strife thy peace is strangely wrought;
If the lion in us pray—thou answerest the lamb.

GEORGE MACDONALD (1824–1905)
From C. S. Lewis, *George MacDonald: An Anthology* (New York: Touchstone Books, Simon & Schuster
　　Trade, 1996), 137. Used by permission of HarperCollins Publishers.

Prayer of a Mother

O our God, grant us the grace to seek first the kingdom of God. Let this quest be our first thought on waking, our last before sleeping. Let it govern all our decisions, all our plans concerning the education of our children, the choice of their vocation, getting them established. Let it decide the orientation of our life; let it occupy the central place. . . . O our heavenly Father, we confess to thee our faithlessness. Teach us to receive everything from thee and hear us in the name of our Lord, Jesus Christ. Amen.

MADAME MIRABAUD (1827–1893)
From Chapal and Pellegrin, *La tradition calvinienne*, 65. © Editions C.L.D. 1981. Used by permission.

A Christmas Prayer of Adoration

Lord Jesus, Redeemer and Savior of humanity, Only Begotten of the Father, shining Morning Star, Sun of Righteousness, we thank thee that thou hast appeared in our darkness and that thy radiant splendor will never set. The patriarchs hoped in thee; Abraham rejoiced to see thy day; the sages awaited thee; the holy prophets foretold thy coming; sages from the east and the shepherds of Bethlehem appeared at thy manger; the heavenly hosts sang at thy birth; apostles, martyrs and saints have repeated the song of the angels, and with them thy church glorifies and praises thee, in all languages and tongues, as her King and Lord.

Thy compassion be praised. Thy mercy be praised. Thy grace be praised forever. Amen.

J. H. GUNNING (1829–1905)
From *Gebeden voor het Huisgezin* (Prayers for the household), 2d edition (Utrecht: G.H.A. Ruys, 1908), 86. Translated by Stanley W. Bamberg and James E. Davison.

Prayer for a Sense of Completeness in Life

Tie the strings to my life, my Lord,
  Then I am ready to go!
Just a look at the horses—
  Rapid! That will do!
Put me in on the firmest side,
  So I shall never fall,
For we must ride to the Judgment,
  And it's partly down hill.
But never I mind the bridges,
  And never I mind the sea;
Held fast in everlasting race
  By my own choice and thee.
Good-by to the life I used to live,
  And the world I used to know;
And kiss the hills for me, just once;
  Now I am ready to go!

EMILY DICKINSON (1830–1886)
From Emily Dickinson, *Selected Poems and Letters of Emily Dickinson* (New York: Doubleday & Co., 1959),
  81–82. Used by permission.

Prayer of Commitment

Father, I bring thee not myself—
  that were the little load;
I bring thee the imperial heart
  I had not strength to hold.
The heart I cherished in my own
  Till mine too heavy grew,
Yet strangest, heavier since it went,
  Is it too large for you?

EMILY DICKINSON (1830–1886)
From Emily Dickinson, *Selected Poems and Letters of Emily Dickinson* (New York: Doubleday & Co., 1959),
  79. Used by permission.

Prayer for the Sabbath

King of Kings, and Lord of Lords, to whom every knee must bow and every tongue confess, how fearful and wonderful are thy works among the children of men! Thou reignest over thine enemies in clouds and darkness, in righteousness and judgment. When thou takest vengeance on them, they are confounded, and tremble, and melt as wax at thy presence. Thou reignest, also, over them that love thee in grace and peace. Thou preservest the souls of thy saints, and deliverest them from the hand of the wicked. Thou givest them light and direction in times of perplexity and trouble, and fillest their hearts with gladness. Thou hast done marvelous things in their behalf. For all these things, O Lord, we desire to rejoice, and to sing a new song unto thee. Our hearts will be glad before thee, and we will make a joyful noise to the Rock of our salvation.

We bless thee for this day which thou hast given us to call these wonders of thy mercy to our remembrance. O enable us to count it honourable, and to devote it to thy holy work. May it be a day of thy right hand and of delight to our souls. May it add strength to our hatred of evil, and love of holiness, and make us walk more determinedly by faith and not by sight. O deliver us from the pollution, the power, and the punishment of sin, through the righteousness of our Redeemer, and the grace of our Sanctifier; and may all our sabbaths on earth tend to fit us the more effectually for the endless sabbath, which the ransomed of the Lord enjoy in heaven. May much bread be cast on the waters and much seed be sown in good ground this day, and many hungry souls be satisfied with the goodness of thy house. May all that preach, all that hear, and all that read thy word, feel its power, and live as it directs. O send forth into all lands and make thy salvation extend to the ends of the earth. Bless thine own work everywhere, that many may rejoice when thou comest to judge the world in righteousness, and the people in equity, by Jesus Christ. Amen.

ALEXANDER WHYTE (1836–1921)
From *Family Worship* (1891), 590.

Prayer of Complete Surrender to God

Use me then, my Saviour, for whatever purpose, and in whatever way, Thou mayest require. Here is my poor heart, an empty vessel; fill it with Thy grace. Here is my sinful and troubled soul; quicken it and refresh it with Thy love. Take my heart for Thine abode; my mouth to spread abroad the glory of Thy name; my love and all my powers, for the advancement of Thy believing people; and never suffer the steadfastness and confidence of my faith to abate—that so at all times I may be enabled from the heart to say, "Jesus needs me, and I Him."

DWIGHT L. MOODY (1837–1899)
From H. E. Fosdick, *The Meaning of Prayer* (New York: Follett Publishing Co., 1949), 52–53.

Morning Prayer Song

O, our dear God,
we have just gotten up from our bed
and we ask you kindly:
Let us be reverent before you—
reverent and obedient —
and let us love one another.
Amen.

JAN KARAFIÁT (1846–1929). This daily morning prayer is an important part of Karafiát's famous children's story "Broucci," (The fireflies), first published in 1876, which became the most popular children's book in the modern Czech Protestant Christian tradition. It is loved by adults as well as children.

Translated by Martin Prudký from Evangelical Church of Czech Brethren, *Evangelický Zpěvník* (Hymnbook) (1979), no. 220. Used by permission.

Prayer for Right
Disposition toward Others

Dear Lord, take out of our hearts all bitterness, hatred, and even indifference, unconcern, as it respects others. Help us to feel kindly toward others, to be sincerely interested in their welfare and happiness. The Lord Jesus was interested in everybody, wanted to help everybody, felt kindly toward everybody. There was never any bitterness, or hatred, or indifference towards those with whom he was daily thrown in contact. Love, true love, unselfish love, love that suffereth long and is kind, was ever to the front, was ever actively in evidence. Grant that it may also be true of all of us in all our relations and contact with others. It is his beautiful spirit that we need to catch, and carry with us all through life.

FRANCIS J. GRIMKÉ (1850–1937)

From Francis J. Grimké, *Stray Thoughts and Meditations*, vol. 3 of *The Works of Francis James Grimké*, edited by Carter G. Woodson (Washington D. C.: Associated Publishers, 1942), 502. Copyright by Associated Publishers. Used by permission.

Prayer of Petition

Let them that love Thy Name be joyful in Thee.—Psalm 5:11

Most gracious Father, we lift up our hearts unto Thee, from Whom alone comes our strength. Help us to trust Thee so wholly that we trust Thee in the dark. Thy mercies are fresh every morning and renewed to us every night. Help us to praise Thee for Thy goodness and to rest in Thy love. Thou knowest what we have need of before we ask Thee. Grant us all that Thou seest we need. Save us from suffering and want, from sickness and misery, from doubt and perplexity, from temptation and sin. Teach us that Thou carest for us, and nothing can harm us or separate us from Thy love. Relieve us from anxiety and fear, that our minds may be at leisure from themselves to soothe and sympathize. Make us useful in the world in which Thou hast placed us, and zealous in service to Thee. Forgive us our sins, in Jesus Christ; give us Thy Spirit to dwell within us, and grant us the joy of conscious communion with Thee. Conform us ever more closely to Thine image as Thou hast revealed it to us in Jesus Christ; lead us in the paths of holiness; and take us at last unto Thyself to dwell forever in Thy presence, the recipients of Thy favor and love. And all we ask, we ask in the Name and for the sake of Thy Son, Jesus Christ our Lord. Amen.

BENJAMIN B. WARFIELD (1851–1921)
From *God's Minute* (Philadelphia: VIR Publishers, 1916), 75.

The Wings of Prayer

Our Father, Thy children who know Thee delight themselves in Thy presence. We are never happier than when we are near Thee. We have found a little heaven in prayer. It has eased our load to tell Thee of its weight; it has relieved our wound to tell Thee of its smart; it has restored our spirit to confess to Thee its wanderings. No place like the mercy seat for us.

We thank Thee, Lord, that we have not only found benefit in prayer, but in the answers to it we have been greatly enriched. Thou hast opened Thy hid treasure to the voice of prayer; Thou hast supplied our necessities as soon as we have cried unto Thee; yea, we have found it true: "Before they call, I will answer, and while they are yet speaking, I will hear."

We do bless Thee, Lord, for instituting the blessed ordinance of prayer. What could we do without it, and we take great shame to ourselves that we should use it so little.

And now, at this hour, wilt Thou hear the voice of our supplications. First, we ask at Thy hands, great Father, complete forgiveness for all our trespasses and shortcomings.

And then, Lord, we have another mercy to ask which shall be the burden of our prayer. It is that Thou wouldest help us to live such lives as pardoned men should do. We have but a little time to tarry here, for our life is but a vapour; soon it vanishes away; but we are most anxious that we may spend the time of our sojourning here in holy fear, that grace may be upon us from the commencement of our Christian life even to the earthly close of it.

Oh! help us. Spirit of the living God, continue still to travail in us. Let the groanings that cannot be uttered, be still within our Spirit, for these are growing pains, and we shall grow while we can sigh and cry, while we can confess and mourn; yet this is not without a blessed hopefulness that He that hath begun a good work in us will perfect it in the day of Christ. Amen.

CHARLES SPURGEON (1834–1892)
From *Prayers from a Metropolitan Pulpit* (New York: Fleming H. Revell, 1906), 76–77.

Prayer after a Sermon

O Lord Jesus, I have tried to preach Thee this morning, but I cannot look with Thine eye. Thou must look on erring ones Thyself. Look, Saviour! Look, sinner! "There is life in a look *at* the crucified One," because there is life in a look *from* the crucified One. May Jesus look, and the sinner look! Amen.

CHARLES SPURGEON (1834–1892)
From *Sermons of Reverend C. H. Spurgeon of London* (New York: Funk & Wagnalls Co., n.d.), vol. 19, 299.

❧ The Twentieth Century

The twentieth century has been a time of ecumenical inclusiveness as the church of Jesus Christ became truly international. The prayers of this century come from a variety of national sources. In addition to the prayers from Europe and America, there are prayers from Japan, Korea, Brazil, and various parts of Africa. Many of the people included in this section were born in the nineteenth century but spent much of their creative energy in the twentieth century. They are bridge people who saw tremendous changes in their lives. The first three persons whose prayers are included, for example, were all born while slavery was still legal in the United States.

Henry van Dyke (1852–1933) was a literary and liturgical scholar who served as pastor of Brick Presbyterian Church in New York and as professor of English literature at Princeton University. Woodrow Wilson (1856–1924) was a close friend of van Dyke and appointed him as minister to the Netherlands. Wilson, both the son and grandson of Presbyterian ministers, served as president of Princeton, governor of New Jersey, and President of the United States. Walter Rauschenbusch (1861–1918) was a Baptist who, as the leading proponent of the social gospel, was one of the greatest Calvinists of the century. Robert E. Speer (1867–1947), an ecumenical pioneer and advocate for world evangelism, was for forty-six years Secretary of the Board of Foreign Missions of the Presbyterian Church in the U.S.A. His little book *Five Minutes a Day* was first compiled for his own daily prayer time.

Hugh Thomson Kerr (1871–1950) was a prominent Presbyterian pastor best known as the author of the hymn "God of Our Life, Through All the Circling Years." Harry Emerson Fosdick (1878–1969) is best known as the pastor of Riverside Church in New York City and a leading modernist. Olive Wyon (1881–1966) was an English Reformed leader of the ecumenical movement who was a pioneer in the development of a Protestant religious order of Reformed women, the Grandchamp Community. Marc Boegner (1881–1970) was the leader of the Reformed Church in France for over two decades and a major figure in the founding of the World Council of Churches.

John Baillie (1886–1960) was an outstanding Scottish theologian and church leader who was moderator of the General Assembly of the Church of Scotland and a president of the World Council of Churches. Karl Barth (1886–1968) was the single most influential theologian of the century. He was born in Switzerland, taught in Germany, and was dismissed because of his refusal to take an oath of allegiance to Hitler. He returned to Switzerland to teach and write. Donald Baillie (1887–1954), John's brother, was a preacher, theologian, and ecumenical leader who taught systematic theology at St. Andrews University in Scotland. Toyohiko Kagawa (1888–1960), a Japanese Presbyterian who organized the first labor union in Japan, was an evangelist in the slums of Kobe and sought to be a peacemaker even in the terrible events of World War II. Eduard Thurneysen (1888–1974), a close friend of Karl Barth, was a Swiss pastor who concluded his career as pastor of the cathedral church in Basel. Josef Hromádka (1889–1969) was a Czech church leader and theologian best known for his efforts to deal sympathetically with Marxism when it took over the government of his country. He was a pioneer in the world ecumenical movement. John A. Mackay (1889–1983) was a Presbyterian missionary statesman, an ecumenist, and president of Princeton Theological Seminary.

André Schlemmer (1890–1973), a medical doctor, was on the committees that prepared the hymnal and the liturgy of the Reformed Church of France in the 1960s. Dora Jackson (c. 1890–1985) was a Pima Indian who was converted and loved to pray. Suzanne de Dietrich (1891–1981) was a writer, biblical scholar, and ecumenical leader of the World Student Christian Federation and the World Council of Churches. Reinhold Niebuhr (1892–1971) was the leading proponent of neo-orthodox theology in the United States. He was a German Reformed pastor who, as professor of ethics at Union Theological Seminary in New York, became very influential in theological and political thought. Corrie ten Boom (1892–1980) was a Dutch woman who resisted the Nazi occupation of her country and sheltered Jews who were trying to escape the death camps. She was, herself, sent to a concentration camp. Kornelis Heiko Miskotte (1894–1976) was a Dutch Reformed pastor who taught theology throughout his career. Two of his books were published in the United States. George F. MacLeod (1895–1991) was an important Scottish church leader who spoke for the marginalized and concluded his career by founding the Iona Community.

Ki-Chul Joo (1897–1944) was one of the most eloquent of the Korean Christian martyrs during the Japanese occupation of his country. Willem A. Visser 't Hooft (1900–1985), a Dutch Reformed leader, was General Secretary of the World Council of Churches from its founding in 1948 until 1965. Shungnak Luke Kim (1902–1989) was a Korean Presbyterian who came to Los Angeles to serve as pastor of the first Korean Presbyterian church in the United States. Peter Marshall (1902–1949) was an influential pastor and preacher best known for the prayers he offered as chaplain of the United States Senate.

Rachel Henderlite (1905–1991) was the first woman to be ordained as a minister in the Presbyterian Church in the United States. Francis Akanu Ibiam (1906–1995) was a Nigerian physician and political leader who served the Presbyterian Church of Nigeria in several capacities including that of president of the All-Africa Church Conference. William Barclay (1907–1978), a Scot, did more than any other scholar to popularize biblical critical scholarship with his *Daily Study Bible*. Lawrence W. Bottoms (1908–1994) was the first African American moderator of the General Assembly of the Presbyterian Church in the United States. John Oliver Nelson (1909–1990) is remembered by Yale Divinity School graduates for his pastoral presence there, and by many others as founder of the Kirkridge Center. Henri Capieu (1909–1993) served as secretary of the French Student Christian Federation and as editor of the hymnal of the Reformed Church of France. Lazarus Lamilami (1910–1977) was the first Australian Aboriginal minister to be ordained by the Uniting Church in Australia. Thomas A. Patterson (1910–1991) was a minister and moderator of the General Assembly of the Presbyterian Church in Ireland who worked for peace and reconciliation between Protestants and Catholics. James A. Jones (1911–1966) was pastor of the Myers Park Presbyterian Church of

Charlotte, North Carolina, and president of Union Theological Seminary in Virginia. Catherine Marshall (1914–1984) edited books by and about her late husband, Peter, but also became well known and beloved for her novels and writings about prayer, and for her lectures and conferences. Kapinga Esetê (d. 1975) was a member of the Presbyterian Church in Zaire and a leader in women's organizations.

The international character of these people indicates the spread of the Reformed movement around the world. The fruit of that missionary movement flowered in the early decades of the twentieth century. The presence of a significant number of women authors is witness to the changing role of women in the church. Toward the middle of the century, women began to be accepted by various Reformed denominations as ministers of the Word and Sacrament. Language about God did not change much with these pioneer women, but they paved the way for those who would follow. Ecumenism is an important theme for the prayer writers of this century. To a considerable degree the ecumenical movement was the fruit of world mission, for it was on the mission field that Christian missionaries discovered the need to work together for the good of the gospel. The prayers of this century also show a deep commitment on the part of many of the writers to issues of justice and peace. The social gospel, staunchly espoused by faculty members at Union Theological Seminary in New York and other seminaries, spread its influence in Christian communions throughout the world. Voices from the Reformed family played a central role in this movement.

Prayer for Lent

O merciful Father, who in compassion for thy sinful children didst send thy Son Jesus Christ to be the Saviour of the world: grant us grace to feel and to lament our share in the evil which made it needful for him to suffer and to die for our salvation. Help us by self-denial, prayer, and meditation to prepare our hearts for deeper penitence and a better life. And give us a true longing to be free from sin, through the deliverance wrought by Jesus Christ, our only Redeemer.

HENRY VAN DYKE (1852–1933)
From World Student Christian Federation, *Venite Adoremus II*, 62. Used by permission of the World Student Christian Federation, Geneva.

Prayer for Peoples and Rulers

Almighty God, Ruler of all peoples of the earth: Forgive, we beseech thee, our shortcomings as a nation; purify our hearts to see and love truth; give wisdom to our counselors and steadfastness to our people; and bring us at last to that fair city of peace whose foundations are mercy, justice, and good-will, and whose Builder and Maker thou art; through thy Son, Jesus Christ our Lord.

WOODROW WILSON (1856–1924)
From John Wallace Suter, *Prayers for a New World* (New York: Charles Scribner's Sons, 1964), 24.

This Earth, Our Home

O God, we thank you for this earth, our home;
for the wide sky and the blessed sun,
for the salt sea and the running water,
for the everlasting hills and the never-resting winds,
for trees and the common grass underfoot.

We thank you for our senses by which we hear the song of birds,
and see the splendor of the summer fields,
and taste of the autumn fruits,
and rejoice in the feel of the snow,
and smell the breath of the spring.

Grant us a heart wide open to all this beauty;
and save our souls from being so blind
that we pass unseeing when even the common thornbush
is aflame with your glory,
O God our creator,
who lives and reigns for ever and ever.

WALTER RAUSCHENBUSCH (1861–1918)

From Jered Kieling, ed., *The Gift of Prayer: A Treasury of Personal Prayer from the World's Spiritual Traditions*, 36. Copyright © 1995 by The Fellowship in Prayer. Reprinted with the permission of The Continuum Publishing Group.

For Womanhood

O God, our Father, we thank Thee that Thine only-begotten Son took our nature upon Him and was born of a Virgin, that He grew up under a mother's loving care and that on His cross He made sure of a home for her with His dearest friend. We thank Thee for His constant tenderness toward all women and for His first meeting on the Resurrection morning. We thank Thee for His influence through all the centuries in protecting women from wrong, in securing justice and equality, in opening the paths of service. And we thank Thee for the faith and devotion with which women in all ages and in all lands have answered Thy love in Him, and in fidelity and sacrifice fulfilled Thy will. Wherever they still suffer injustice and wrong we pray Thee to deliver them. Wherever their power is wasted on inferior ends, recall them to their great mission. Help them as they mould the future in the child life that is in their care, to believe in the possibility of Thy Kingdom and to train for its citizenship that which Thou hast entrusted to them, in the Name of Thy Holy Child Jesus.

ROBERT E. SPEER (1867–1947)

From *Five Minutes a Day*, 324. Copyright 1943 by The Westminster Press. Used by permission of Westminster John Knox Press.

For Humility

O God our Father, deliver us from the foolishness of self-confidence, from all boasting and vanity, from pride of energy and false notions of success. Teach us that our springs are not in ourselves but in Thee, that so far from being able to do what we will, we can neither will nor do any good except by Thy grace and with Thy help, that it is when we are weak in ourselves that we are strong in Thee, that Thy power is made perfect in our conscious lack of power that compels us to lay our helplessness on Thy strength. Here may we find our rest and feel, pouring through all our impotence, the tides of Thy mighty Spirit, for Thine is the kingdom, the power and glory.

ROBERT E. SPEER (1867–1947)

From *Five Minutes a Day*, 280. Copyright 1943 by The Westminster Press. Used by permission of Westminster John Knox Press.

Prayer for All of Life

God of our life, through all the circling years,
We trust in Thee;
In all the past, through all our hopes and fears,
Thy hand we see.
With each new day, when morning lifts the veil,
We own Thy mercies, Lord, which never fail.

God of the past, our times are in Thy hand;
With us abide.
Lead us by faith to hope's true promised land;
Be Thou our guide.
With Thee to bless, the darkness shines as light,
And faith's fair vision changes into sight.

God of the coming years, through paths unknown
We follow thee;
When we are strong, Lord, leave us not alone;
Our refuge be.
Be Thou for us in life our daily bread.
Our heart's true home when all our years have sped.

HUGH THOMSON KERR (1871–1950)

From Presbyterian Church (U.S.A.), *The Presbyterian Hymnal* (1990), no. 275. Copyright, 1928, by F. M.
Braselman; renewed 1956 by Presbyterian Board of Christian Education. Used by permission of Westminster John Knox Press.

Prayer for Courage

Eternal Spirit, from whom we come and to whom we belong, and in whose service is our peace, we worship thee.

Lift us up, we beseech thee, from cowardice to courage. Save us from self-pity. Recover us from our whimpering complaints. Lo, we are the sons and daughters of soldiers who fought a good fight before they fell on sleep, and were not afraid. Build into us also stout hearts, that we in our generation may stand undaunted by fear, unconquered by adversity, unstained by cowardice.

Lift us up, we pray thee, from vindictiveness to goodwill. If we are harboring grudges, if hatefulness has taken hold of our spirits, save us, we pray thee, from such a desecration of this holy hour. Bring sympathy back to us, and understanding and the fair grace to put ourselves in others' places before we judge them.

Lift us up above malice and evil-speaking and unkindness of heart. Arouse in us the spirit of Christ, who could pray upon the cross for those who put him there. O God, help us to be Christians in our hearts because love is there.

Lift us, we pray thee, from selfishness to service. Remind us of downcast and stricken lives. Let our imaginations run out into our prisons, the houses where the poor lie down in cold and penury, the asylums where disordered minds beat themselves out against their vain imaginings, the unprivileged areas of our city's life and of the world where blessings that we take for granted are little known, and hunger stalks and fear haunts and tomorrow is full of terror. Wake up within us, we beseech thee, our forgotten kindliness.

And with all this, Spirit of the eternal Christ, lift us up from doubt to faith. Lift us out of our cynicism, our skepticism, our unwillingness to believe that the good may be true, into a courageous faith and certitude concerning God and divine purposes. Illumine us, thou Sun of the morning, until not only shall our mountain peaks shine with a new confidence, but the very valleys shall feel thy noontime's splendor and we have faith again in ourselves, in others, and in thee.

We pray in the Spirit of Christ. Amen.

HARRY EMERSON FOSDICK (1878–1969)

From Leo S. Thorne, ed., *Prayers from Riverside*, 62–63. © 1983 The Pilgrim Press. Used by permission of the publisher.

Holy Communion

LORD, this is Thy feast,
prepared by Thy longing,
spread at Thy command,
attended at Thine invitation,
blessed by Thine own word,
distributed by Thine own hand,
the undying memorial of Thy sacrifice upon the Cross,
the full gift of Thine everlasting love,
and its perpetuation till time shall end.
LORD, this is the Bread of heaven,
Bread of life,
that, whoso eateth, never shall hunger more.
And this the Cup of pardon, healing, gladness, strength,
that, whoso drinketh, thirsteth not again.
So may we come, O Lord, to Thy Table:
Lord Jesus, come to us.

OLIVE WYON (1881–1966)

From *The Altar Fire* (Philadelphia: Westminster Press, 1954), 80. Used by permission of Westminster John Knox Press, Louisville, Ky., and SCM Press, Ltd., London.

Blessed Are the Pure in Heart

Today again, O Lord, I want to feed on this word, one of the most beautiful that Christ ever spoke. He knew the ineffable joy of feeling himself to be in perfect communion with you, because no soiled spot ever tarnished the purity of his heart. To be among those for whom all things become new because the old stains are forever past; to be a new creation in Christ: my God, that is the earnest expectation of my heart, but I know that I am weak and tottering. I will never overcome unless I surrender myself without reservation to your action.

With you I must will the final liberations; by you I must be made able to accept them. Strengthen me against myself, O my God! I have not been completely conquered!

MARC BOEGNER (1881–1970)
From Chapal and Pellegrin, *La tradition calvinienne*, 67. © Editions C.L.D. 1981. Used by permission.

For Unity of Soul

My God, you read my heart. . . . Forgive me for my shortcomings, break my resistance, make me able to want with a steady will what I too often want only with intermittent desire. I well know from frequent experience—for which I give you thanks—that to live in communion with you is the only true life, outside of which all that men live for can only sink sooner or later into death. But I still find in me divergent desires, contradictory wills. Unity is not yet achieved—and you alone can give it to me.

MARC BOEGNER (1881–1970)
From Chapal and Pellegrin, *La tradition calvinienne*, 68. © Editions C.L.D. 1981. Used by permission.

True Christian Graces

O Thou in whose boundless being are laid up all the treasures of wisdom and truth, and holiness, grant that through constant fellowship with thee the true graces of Christian character may more and more take shape within my soul:
The grace of a thankful and uncomplaining heart:
The grace to await thy leisure patiently and to answer Thy call promptly:
The grace of courage whether in suffering or in danger:
The grace to endure hardness as a good soldier of Jesus Christ:
The grace of boldness in standing for what is right:
The grace of preparedness, lest I enter into temptation:
The grace of bodily discipline:
The grace of strict truthfulness:
The grace to treat others as I would have others treat me:
The grace of charity, that I may refrain from hasty judgment:
The grace of silence, that I may refrain from hasty speech:
The grace of forgiveness towards all who have wronged me:
The grace of tenderness towards all who are weaker than myself:
The grace of steadfastness in continuing to desire that thou wilt do as now I pray.

JOHN BAILLIE (1886–1960)

From *A Diary of Private Prayer* (New York: Charles Scribner's Sons, 1949), 55. Used by permission of Simon & Schuster, New York, and Oxford University Press, Oxford.

Christmas Prayer for All People

O Lord, our God, when we are afraid do not let us despair. When we are disappointed do not let us become bitter. When we fall do not let us remain prostrate. When we are at the end of our understanding and our powers, do not let us then perish. No, let us feel then Thy nearness and Thy love, which Thou hast promised especially to those whose hearts are humble and broken and who stand in fear before Thy word. To all men Thy Son has come as to those who are so beset. Indeed, because we are all so beset he was born in a stable and died on a cross. Lord, awaken us all and keep us all awake to this knowledge and to this confession.

And now we think of all the darkness and suffering of this our time; . . . of all the burdens that so many must bear uncomforted. . . . We think of the sick and the sick in spirit, the poor, the displaced, the oppressed, those who suffer injustice, the children who have no parents or no proper parents. And we think of all who are called to help . . . the judges and officials, the teachers and leaders of youth, the men and women who are responsible for writing books and newspapers, the doctors and nurses in the hospitals, those who proclaim Thy word in the various churches and congregations near at hand and far away. We think of them all with the petition that the light of Christmas may shine brightly for them and for us, much more brightly than before, that thereby they and we may be helped. We ask all this in the name of the Savior in whom Thou hast already heard us and wilt hear us again and again. Amen.

KARL BARTH (1886–1968)

From Karl Barth, *Selected Prayers*, translated by Keith R. Crim (Richmond: John Knox Press, 1965), 22–23. © M. E. Bratcher 1965. German original title: *Gebete*, © Theologischer Verlag Zürich. Used by permission of Theologischer Verlag Zürich.

Year's End

O Lord, our God! Our years come and go. And we ourselves live and die. But Thou art and remainest the same. Thy dominion and Thy faithfulness, Thy righteousness and Thy mercy, have no beginning and no end. And thus Thou art the origin and the goal even of our lives, Thou art the judge of our thoughts, words, and deeds.

We are grieved that today we can only confess that even to this hour we have so often and ever anew forgotten, denied, and offended Thee. But today we are illumined and comforted by the word through which Thou hast given us to know that Thou art our Father and we are Thy children because Thy dear Son, Jesus Christ, for our sakes has become man, has died and risen again, and is our brother.

We thank Thee for the privilege now, on the last Sunday of the year, of once again proclaiming and hearing these glad tidings. Do Thou Thyself make us free to say that which is right and also to hear it aright, that this hour may serve Thy glory and bring to us all peace and well-being. Amen.

KARL BARTH (1886–1968)

From Karl Barth, *Selected Prayers*, translated by Keith R. Crim (Richmond: John Knox Press, 1965), 24.
© M. E. Bratcher 1965. German original title: *Gebete*, © Theologischer Verlag Zürich. Used by permission of Theologischer Verlag Zürich.

For Openness to God's Leading

Eternal God, who hast set before us life and death for our choice, and hast given us Jesus Christ to be the way, the truth, and the life; help us to enter that way, to receive that truth, and to live by that life. Suffer us not to miss the purpose of our creation, but make us to be sons and daughters of thine and servants of thy kingdom. Through the same Jesus Christ our Lord.

DONALD BAILLIE (1887–1954)
From World Student Christian Federation, *Venite Adoremus II*, 131. Used by permission of the World Student Christian Federation, Geneva.

The Burden

Take Thou the burden, Lord;
I am exhausted with this heavy load.
  My tired hands tremble,
  And I stumble, stumble
    Along the way.
Oh, lead with Thine unfailing arm
  Again today.

Unless Thou lead me, Lord,
The road I journey on is all too hard.
Through trust in Thee alone
  Can I go on.

Yet not for self alone
Thus do I groan;
My people's sorrows are the load I bear.
  Lord, hear my prayer—
  May Thy strong hand
    Strike off all chains
  That load my well-loved land.
  God, draw her close to Thee!

TOYOHIKO KAGAWA (1888–1968)
From Toyohiko Kagawa, *Songs from the Slums*, 89–90. Copyright 1935; renewed 1963. Used by permission
  of Abingdon Press.

Prayer of Expectation

Lord Jesus, we want to be people who watch, who expect your coming; we want to grow in you, to be among those in whom the power of your hope is at work and who confess you in word and in deed. Awaken us, Lord. Do not let us sleep. You speak your powerful word always anew throughout the ages. Give us ears to hear! Amen.

EDUARD THURNEYSEN (1888–1974). An adapted version of this prayer was included as a
  prayer for illumination in the liturgy of the Reformed Church of France in 1963.
From Chapal and Pellegrin, *La tradition calvinienne*, 69. © Editions C.L.D. 1981. Used by permission.

In Times of Struggle and Suffering

O Lord, our God, you created the heavens and the earth and you govern them in the perfection of your holy thoughts. But now sin and great suffering are in the world, and death reigns over us because we do not want to understand your thoughts. Grant us wills that are right and lift the veil from our eyes so that we may see you as your Son Jesus Christ taught us to see you, and so may keep ourselves, in you, in silence and expectation. Amen.

EDUARD THURNEYSEN (1888–1974)
From Chapal and Pellegrin, *La tradition calvinienne*, 70. © Editions C.L.D. 1981. Used by permission.

Pastoral Prayer for the Congregation

Let us bow humbly to our God and call on Him together:
LORD, our God and Father in Jesus Christ, we honor you with all our hearts, because you are the Holy One and all the world can not comprehend your glory. We are coming to you in hopeful confidence, because you come ahead to meet us and to deliver us from all that makes us estranged from you. You sent your Son in order for him to take our place where we dwell in our frailty and powerlessness, in our sin and corruption. We thank you for the grace that we can be counted among the crowd of sinners who put all their hope in you. Please, don't let us be without your word; speak to us, so that everyone will personally hear your voice, and will understand your word and will receive it as light for life's journey. Forgive us, O Lord, forgive us that we have hardened our hearts so many times to your beckoning voice. You never leave us without your promises. Your hand is stretched to-

ward us all the time, but our deceitful and corrupt hearts try to pull away from you and follow our own ideas.

At this moment, gathered in order to be taught by your word, we beseech you humbly for the Holy Spirit—for the light of your truth and the dew of your mercy. Pass through us as through your people. Take away everything which separates us from you and from our fellows. Confirm us in your truth and fill us with the spirit of unity and love. Take every one of us, personally, chisel us and fit us as living stones into the construction of your temple, into the community of your church! Take the burden of our concerns and grief, our sorrow and troubles, helplessness and illness from us. We are placing our confidence only in you. Only in you do we hope, only for you do we wait in expectation.

Bless our congregation, answer in mercy our intimate questions, and ally us with all those who are not with us today, but desire to be gathered in the community of your people. Hear us in the name of Jesus Christ! Amen.

JOSEF L. HROMÁDKA (1889–1969)
Translated by Martin Prudký from Evangelical Church of Czech Brethren, *Sbírka kázání* (Sermon collection) (Prague, 1993), 34–35. Used by permission.

In His Light
May We See Light

Oh thou who dwellest in the light that is unapproachable and full of glory, who in the fullness of time didst send thy Son who is the light of the world, in His light may we see light clearly. In His light may we see the majesty of thy being and the graciousness of thy purpose. In His light may we see our world and understand it, in this the time in which our lot is cast.

To that end bless us as we assemble together here seeking thy light upon our work. Graciously grant, O lord of light and glory, that this journal may ever be loyal to thy truth and to thy gracious purpose for the world, and may it too be ever relevant to the time in which we live and to its challenge. May the Holy Spirit of truth lead us into all truth. And may the grace of our Lord Jesus Christ, who is light and life and the way to both, graciously grant us a sense of His luminous presence that we may truly be guided in all our deliberations, whether to analyze or to decide, whether to explore thy will or to be challenged by human need, in the name of Him who taught us to pray when we say: Our Father, who art in Heaven . . .

JOHN A. MACKAY (1889–1983). This prayer was offered by Dr. Mackay as president emeritus of Princeton Theological Seminary and honorary chairman of the Editorial Council of *Theology Today* at its meeting in Princeton on April 14, 1961. The motto of the journal at that time and until 1990, given to it by Dr. Mackay, was "Our life in God's light." Used by permission of William O. Harris.

For the Sick and for Doctors

Lord, our God, we commit to you the sick and the infirm, children who suffer, men and women unable to work, the elderly with failing strength, and all those in agony. Enlighten and sustain them, so that in faith they may find some meaning for their suffering and commit themselves to you. Deliver them in your mercy.

Have pity on those who suffer lack of nervous equilibrium, and even in the midst of mental illness, let your light shine.

Sustain and guide those to whom you have entrusted the care of the sick and those who watch over the health of their neighbors. Give to the men and women whom you have called into the medical profession, as well as to their assistants, devotion, tact, and discernment. Let theirs be healing hands; give them the look that encourages, the word that consoles.

ANDRÉ SCHLEMMER (1890–1973). Liturgy of the Reformed Church of France, 1963.
From Chapal and Pellegrin, *La tradition calvinienne*, 80. © Editions C.L.D. 1981. Used by permission.

Twenty-third Psalm

Thank you, Father, for the sheep. Thank you for being our Shepherd just like the shepherds of the flocks when David was a shepherd boy. David came back and wrote all those beautiful psalms like the first psalm, which is so helpful. Father, O, how we thank you for the Twenty-third Psalm. "The Lord is my shepherd, I shall not want. . . ." Sometimes, Father, when I am sitting here I call on you and you hear me. Help me, Father, to be a blessing to someone. I'm a poor soul but I know that you hear me. Thank you for supplying my needs. Amen.

DORA JACKSON (Pima) (c. 1890–1985)
Used by permission of the Session, First Presbyterian Church, Mesa, Arizona.

For Peace and Justice

O Lord, our God, who hast reconciled us to thyself and to one another through the death of thy Son, and hast entrusted to us the ministry of reconciliation, keep ever before our hearts and minds the price that thou hast paid for the salvation of the world. Crucify our pride, destroy our enmities, and let the cross of thy Son bear in us all its fruits of righteousness and peace.

Give us to share his holy indignation in the presence of evil and his merciful love for him who commits it. Help us to forgive, since we live ourselves only in thy forgiveness.

Grant unto thy church the unity of the saints in the bond of peace, that in the midst of the world it may be the authentic messenger of thy grace and pardon. Abolish all the walls of separation which still divide thy children. Hasten the day, O Lord, when all races shall unite in a single song of praise to the glory of thy name.

SUZANNE DE DIETRICH (1891–1981)
From World Student Christian Federation, *Venite Adoremus II*, 149. Used by permission of the World Student Christian Federation, Geneva.

Thanksgiving for Friends

We thank thee, O Lord, for this wonderful gift of friendship. We thank thee for all those whose friendship has been a light on our path.

We pray for our friends; for our comrades in the fight, with whom we are joined in the same faith and the same service; for those who know thee and those who do not yet know thee; for those who are going through times of loneliness, of suffering, or of doubt, and whom we name secretly in our hearts.

We commit one another to thy mercy. Increase our faith; increase our love.

SUZANNE DE DIETRICH (1891–1981)
From World Student Christian Federation, *Venite Adoremus II*, 166. Used by permission of the World Student Christian Federation, Geneva.

For Our Fellow Men

O God, who hast made us a royal priesthood, that we may offer unto thee prayer and intercession for our fellow men, hear us we pray:

For all who labour with their hands, that they may enjoy the rewards of their industry;

For those who bear the responsibilities of leadership and administration, that they may not use their authority and power for selfish advantage but be guided to do justice and to love mercy;

For those who have suffered in the battles of life, through the inhumanity of their fellows, their own limitations, or the incomprehensible forces of evil, that they may contend against injustice without bitterness, overcome their weakness with diligence, and learn to accept with patience what cannot be altered;

For the rulers of the nations, that they may act wisely and without pride, may seek to promote peace among the peoples and establish justice in our common life;

For teachers and ministers of the word, for artists and interpreters of our spiritual life, that they may rightly divide the word of truth, and not be tempted by any ignoble passion to corrupt the truth to which they are committed;

For prophets and saints, who awaken us from sloth, that they may continue to hold their torches high in a world darkened by prejudice and sin, and ever be obedient to the heavenly vision.

O God, who hast bound us together in this bundle of life, give us grace to understand how our lives depend upon the courage, the industry, the honesty, and the integrity of our fellow men, that we may be mindful of their needs, grateful for their faithfulness, and faithful in our responsibilities to them; through Jesus Christ our Lord.

REINHOLD NIEBUHR (1872–1971)

From World Student Christian Federation, *Venite Adoremus II*, 40–41. Used by permission of the World Student Christian Federation, Geneva.

Prayer for Serenity

God, give us serenity to accept what cannot be changed,
courage to change what should be changed,
and wisdom to distinguish the one from the other.

Attributed to REINHOLD NIEBUHR (1892–1971)
From *The Presbyterian Outlook*, Feb. 23, 1970, p. 8. Another version of this prayer in the first person singular ("God, give me the serenity to accept what I cannot change . . ."), used by Alcoholics Anonymous and others, is attributed to an eighteenth-century German Pietist, Friedrich Oetinger (1702–1782) (*The Presbyterian Outlook*, April 13, 1970, p. 2).

Prayer for Patience

Lord, You alone know how much patience I need. Open my eyes when I have difficult times and trials, to help me see them from Your side and to realize that they are meant to teach me patience. Lord Jesus, thank You that You are always with me and that, when I look up, I see You. Everything else becomes small, compared to this joy. Amen.

CORRIE TEN BOOM (1892–1980)
From Corrie ten Boom, *This Day Is the Lord's*, 21. Copyright 1979. Used by permission of Fleming H. Revell, a division of Baker Book House Company.

Prayer for a Sense of God's Closeness

Father, You know that I trust in You. Yet at times it seems as if You are far away. Show me in what respect I depend on somebody or something else, instead of on You only. I know You will always be with me, if I remain close to You. Hallelujah!

CORRIE TEN BOOM (1892–1980)
From Corrie ten Boom, *This Day Is the Lord's*, 111. Copyright 1979. Used by permission of Fleming H. Revell, a division of Baker Book House Company.

Prayer for Divine Guidance

Help me, Lord, to live one day at a time. Thank You that Your grace is sufficient for today and that I don't need to worry about tomorrow, because Your grace will be sufficient for tomorrow also. Father, if You will, You can use even me. Make me willing to be looked upon as foolish by the world, if people should consider me so. Amen.

CORRIE TEN BOOM (1892–1980)
From Corrie ten Boom, *This Day Is the Lord's*, 121. Copyright 1979. Used by permission of Fleming H. Revell, a division of Baker Book House Company.

Praise and Petition to Christ

Eternal thanks to you, Lord of the earth, Lord of this dark earth, that you have dimmed your dazzling light to be light for us, that you have not wished to compete with any power or god but have humbled yourself and taken the form of a servant. . . .
Love, O Love, O marvelous Love,
you are mighty over those who shrink before you.
Strengthen us by your tender hands,
make us great through your smallness,
make us free through your chains,
make us rich through your need,
make us joyous through your suffering,
make us alive through your death,
for yours is the kingdom, and the power and the glory forever.
Amen.

K. H. MISKOTTE (1894–1976)
From *Gevulde Stilte* (Pregnant silence), 10. Kampen: J. H. Kok, 1974. Used by permission of the publisher. Translated by Stanley W. Bamberg and James E. Davison.

Prayer before the Sermon

Lord our God, it is a joy for us, a high privilege, to seek silence on your day—but not an empty silence, not a mystic silence, not a silence of the soul, but the silence of the astonished mind that does not have the strength for it, that does not know where to go with it, that would like to anoint the preacher, and the ground of preaching, with very precious oil as a sign of rediscovery, as a sign that we have understood the new covenant.

O Lord, pour over us the anointing of your Holy Spirit that we may understand things and hold up your things as things of high holiness, distinguishing them from the world.

O Lord, we are in chaos, and the chaos is not only outside us but also and especially within us. We have your law but we cannot earn anything with it. In it we have a guide, but we turn away from it again and again. There is more and more confusion in our life, and in the life of the world, and in our own soul, and in our own thought, in our sleepless nights and in our dull days. We are nowhere any more; and because we are nowhere, we are now here. For that, thanks be to you—that it is permissible and that it is possible. Amen.

K. H. MISKOTTE (1894–1976)

From *Gevulde Stilte* (Pregnant silence), 11. Kampen: J. H. Kok, 1974. Used by permission of the publisher. Translated by Stanley W. Bamberg and James E. Davison.

An Earth Redeemed

When we partake of the living bread and the living vine, our triune God,
help us to know ourselves to have part in an earth redeemed;
Help us to know ourselves to have part in new life blood for the world:
to cling together as branches to the vine,
to give both shade and refreshment to the world.
Help us to be Thy healing spirit in the world
till all shall be pervaded,
So shall we freshly partake:
So shall we freshly purvey:
So shall we freshly be Thy life of love
till Thou shalt come to judge.

God the Creator, Thou hast made the bread.
Christ the Redeemer, Thou hast changed it.
Holy Spirit, the Binder, Thou dost convey it:
bread for our touching, food for our souls:
Even as our lives are bound together in Thee.

God the Creator, Thou hast made the vine.
Christ the Redeemer: Thou hast changed it:
Holy Spirit, the Binder, Thou dost convey it:
the cup from hand to hand, the life blood from heart to heart:
Even as our lives are bound together in Thee.

God the Creator, Thou hast changed us.
Christ, the Redeemer, Thou hast changed us.
Holy Spirit, the Binder, Thou dost keep us changed:
Even as now we are bound together in Thee.

GEORGE F. MACLEOD (1895–1991)
From George F. MacLeod, *The Whole Earth Shall Cry Glory: Iona Prayers* (Glasgow: Wild Goose Publications, 1987), 31. Used by permission of the publisher.

A Martyr's Prayer

My Lord and my shepherd, I have been walking in the shadow of death. The hands of those who desire to kill me are constantly pursuing after me. As I face the coming crisis of death, Lord, give me the courage to overcome the power of death. O God, it has not been easy for me as a fragile human being to endure the never-ending torture. Let me persevere with the sufferings of sword and fire. O God, as I may have to leave my old mother, my wife and my children behind, I trust them into your hands. Since I am no longer able to take responsibility to support them, I pray for your provision that they may not become a burden to anyone, especially to my church. Gracious God, it is for righteousness that I live, and it is my prayer that for righteousness I may die. O Lord, into your hands I want to commit my spirit. As I collapse holding the cross in my hands, hold me in your hands and receive my spirit. Amen.

KI-CHUL JOO (1897–1944)
From *I Will Offer My Blood* (in Korean), 1968. Translated by Park Eung Chun, Assistant Professor of New Testament, San Francisco Theological Seminary. Used by permission.

Prayer of Consecration

Lord, we want to be your instruments. We have nothing to offer you but our desire to be laborers in your harvest. But since
you have chosen the weak things of this world, the things that are
not, will you not choose us, even us, to be your servants? We cannot, of ourselves, bring your message to humankind. Grant us,
we pray, not to speak our own words, but your word by which
men and women may come to know you and to love you.

Grant us courage to confess the name of Jesus Christ before the
world. Help us to take to heart the situation of those around us,
to act as neighbors toward them, to share with them what you
have given us. We do not ask to see the fruits of our labor.
We want only to know that you are using us for your saving
work and that your kingdom is coming among us. Send us, Lord,
as witnesses of the good news of your love revealed in Jesus
Christ. Amen.

WILLEM A. VISSER 'T HOOFT (1900–1985)
From Chapal and Pellegrin, *La tradition calvinienne*, 71. © Editions C.L.D. 1981. Used by permission.

A Pastor's Leave-Taking from a Congregation

We pause this Sunday morning to praise you for bringing us this far
by faith. Though we are still small in numbers, our hearts are full of
gratitude for your goodness in founding us in the first place. As your
humble servant, I thank you for calling me to this congregation as pastor. Twenty-one years later you have seen fit to send me back home to
Korea as president of our nation's oldest Christian university and I
take leave now knowing these have been the best years of my life.

I pray at this moment for this wonderful church family and the
larger Korean American community of which it is a part. Life has not
been easy in this country for our people as they have faced many bar-

riers due to differences in language and culture. Our children have prospered and done well in school because of the sacrifices and hard work of their parents. Many of our mothers have toiled in sewing factories for years and fathers have labored in a variety of menial jobs. Yet they have never complained and have continued to fight the good fight day in and day out for decades. Through it all this church on this corner in South Central Los Angeles has been their rock in a weary land and shelter in the time of storm.

Our people are grateful for this great land of America. It is true we have experienced prejudice and discrimination but we have been given opportunities here that do not exist in our homeland. We appreciate the meaning of freedom and democracy because we were denied them so long during the colonial period and, even now, back there many family members and friends of ours are suffering. Dear Hananim Aboji, please continue to bless America and grant that this nation may one day fulfill all of its highest ideals and noblest dreams.

You call us by name and you know even the number of hairs on our head. Seeing your son Jesus, we see who you are and what you have done for us. In his name we pray this day, in all the days to come, even forevermore. Amen.

SHUNGNAK LUKE KIM (1902–1989)
Translated and used by permission of Warren W. Lee, Professor of Ministry at San Francisco Theological Seminary.

Prayer for Those
Who Serve

Lord Jesus,
Bless all who serve us,
who have dedicated their lives
to the ministry of others—
all the teachers of our schools
who labor so patiently with so little appreciation;
all who wait upon the public,
the clerks in the stores who have to accept criticism,
complaints, bad manners, and selfishness
at the hands of a thoughtless public.
Bless the mailmen, the drivers of streetcars
and buses who must listen to people who
lose their tempers.
Bless every humble soul who, in these
days of stress and strain, preaches sermons
without words. Amen.

PETER MARSHALL (1902–1949)

Prayer of Confession

We come to Thee, O Christ, confessing to Thee the fears that twist our lives and keep us from the inner calm and peace that come from Thee:

The fear of ourselves, that we cannot do what is expected of us;

The fear of being found out for our littleness and pride in ourselves;

The fear of being left out when joy and richness come to others;

The fear of not being ready when opportunities present themselves for service;

The fear of death, that when it comes our time to die, we shall not have done the things we would have done, because we were afraid to venture out.

We find ourselves shrinking back before the unknown, wanting assurance where we must have faith;

We find ourselves hesitating to follow Thee, O Christ, afraid the cost may be too great, and life may pass us by.

Give us the strength and peace that only Thou canst give. Amen.

RACHEL HENDERLITE (1905–1991). Written for a service of worship at Montreat, North Carolina, July 20, 1954.

Prayer from the All Africa Conference of Churches

O God, you who are from generation to generation the Creator of the ends of the earth and all that it contains, we of the continent of Africa bow our heads to you in humble thanks for the work that you have wrought in our lands and communities over the years.

We remember with joy the refuge which your only begotten Son our Saviour and his earthly parents took in Africa. We rejoice when we remember the journey of the Ethiopian eunuch, and his Christian fellowship with your disciple Philip in the Gaza desert.

It is a wonderful tribute to Africa that Simon of Cyrene helped to bear the heavy wooden cross upon which you hung and suffered for us sinners here in Africa and all over the world.

We can never forget the countless men and women of other lands who spread throughout Africa the gospel news of the saving grace of Christ, and now that same call comes to us to do the same.

When we think of these things our gratitude knows no bounds.

FRANCIS AKANU IBIAM (1906–1995)
From John Carden, *With All God's People* (Geneva: WCC Publications, 1989), 191. Used by permission.

A Prayer for St. Andrew's Day

O Lord Jesus, help us to accept your call as Andrew did.
Help us, as Andrew did, to hear your call above the many voices
of the world.
Grant that
    the claims of business;
    the attractions of pleasure;
    the cares of this world
may not make us fail to hear your call.
Help us, as Andrew did, to obey at once; and grant that we may
    not put off until tomorrow that decision which we ought to
    make today.
Help us, as Andrew did, to give ourselves wholly to your obedi-
    ence.
Cleanse us from self-will, which would make us want nothing
    but our own way;
the lack of discipline, which would make us refuse to make the ef-
    fort which obedience demands; the subjection to the fear, or
    the desire for the favour, of men, which would make us refuse
    your commandments;
the love of comfort and security, which would make us take the
    easy rather than the right way. Help us here and now to accept
    your call, that one day we may share your glory. This we ask
    for your love's sake. Amen.

WILLIAM BARCLAY (1907–1978). Saint Andrew's Day is November 30.
From *A Barclay Prayer Book* (London: SCM Press, and Valley Forge, Pa.: Trinity Press International, 1990),
    142–43. Used by permission.

For the Church

O God our Father, we thank you for the church in which this life was nourished. We pray that you will continue to bless this church, that we may become the people who are the community of God, knowing the community that comes from the power of the Holy Spirit. [We pray] that other souls may be nourished, as this soul was, into completeness of life, because they have learned from the church of the Lord Jesus Christ, who helps us to live in this fashion.

We thank you for the church through which we have learned Christian education and through which Evelyn learned Christian education; a church that helps us to know and understand that learning is an interweaving of knowledge and experience and that causes us to realize that the individual must do the weaving. Help us in our weaving. Help us to understand with Evelyn that we work from the back side and that life is like the weaver's shuttle, that it is rough and unsightly, that there are loose ends and threads. But we pray that we may be able to continue working in this fellowship and this community that helps us to live by faith, making it possible for us to weave until the pattern is turned around in the completeness of life, and we begin to look at life from the end toward the beginning.

We thank you for the faith that comes from the church. In this time of history we pray you will continue to be in this church so that it may be the church that leads us to a new faith, a new hope, a new love, and a new horizon. In the name of the Lord Jesus Christ. Amen.

LAWRENCE W. BOTTOMS (1908–1994)

Offered at the funeral of Evelyn L. Green, church educator and leader of Presbyterian Women. Transcribed from audiotape by Marietta Yarnell and used by her permission.

Prayer for Student Life

O Son of Man, teach us to weigh wisely all activities and occasions on campus. Give us a sense of what is important, that we may fruitfully allot our time to our studies, our sports, our clubs, our friends and our church; to the end that we may become true stewards of time and skill, through him of whom it was said that he did all things well, even Jesus Christ our Lord.

JOHN OLIVER NELSON (1909–1990)
From World Student Christian Federation, *Venite Adoremus II*, 106. Used by permission of the World Student Christian Federation, Geneva.

For University Domestic Staff

We thank thee, Lord, for the faithfulness of those who care for this place, serve our food, and ease our life with endless daily chores. Grant to them joy in what they do, and to us grace to show our thankfulness to them and to thee, in Christ.

JOHN OLIVER NELSON (1909–1990)
From World Student Christian Federation, *Venite Adoremus II*, 121. Used by permission of the World Student Christian Federation, Geneva.

Sunday Morning

Lord, we sing to you and give you thanks. For, despite our pains and faults, in the midst of our pains and faults, we know that you are a God whom one can only admire, praise, and love in Jesus Christ.

For the world, so beautiful but so fragile; for life, so lovely but so threatened; for this immense universe in which your kingdom will spread, we praise you.

For this day which speaks to us again of the resurrection, for your church which gathers us together, we praise you.

For your gospel, for our baptism, for our desire to serve you, for the promise of your eternity, we praise you.

And because we can love you and love each other on the earth, in the name of the love of Christ, in peace and with joy, Lord we praise you.

HENRI CAPIEU (1909–1993)
From Chapal and Pellegrin, *La tradition calvinienne*, 84. © Editions C.L.D. 1981. Used by permission.

For Strength through the Day

Great Bunji God,
you sent your Son Jesus
to be our Saviour, our Guide and our Friend.
At the dawn of this new day
we pray for strength to follow in his steps,
and to be true witnesses for him
among our people who love the great earth mother,
your gift to them from the dreamtime.
We pray for all people of all countries,
that they may become one great family
with Jesus as Saviour.
As we come to the evening of this day,
may we go to our rest in the quiet hours of the night
knowing that, in spite of our human weaknesses,
we have truly walked with Jesus.
This prayer we offer in the name of Jesus,
our Good Friend, Amralba.

LAZARUS LAMILAMI (1910–1977)
From Uniting Church in Australia, *Uniting in Worship*, 233. Copyright 1988 the National Commission on
    Liturgy of the Uniting Church in Australia.

Prayer for Peace

We are tired, Lord,
weary of the long night without rest.
We grow complaining and bitter.
We sorrow for ourselves
as we grow hardened to the pain of others.
Another death leaves us unmoved.
A widow's tears fall unnoticed.
Our children know only the bitterness
already possessing their parents.
Our violent words
explode into violent acts
by the hands of youth
bringing destruction without thought or reason.
Lord, have mercy upon us.
Lead us to repentance that we may forgive
and be forgiven. Amen.

THOMAS A. PATTERSON (1910–1991). Thomas A. Patterson was a Presbyterian minister in
    Northern Ireland.
From John Carden, *With All God's People* (Geneva: WCC Publications, 1989), 79. Used by permission of the
    author's daughter, Rev. Ruth Patterson.

A Prayer of Thanksgiving

. . . Our tribute of praise can never match the wondrous measure of thy mercy. Our lips can never express the depth of gratitude which our hearts feel. In thy providence we have been kept, of thy bounty we have partaken, and under the shadow of thy wings our souls have learned to rejoice. Thus far thou hast brought us along the pilgrim-ways of life. Goodness and mercy have followed us all our days. By green pastures we have been led. In the dark valley we have not walked alone. Our comfort has been in thy rod and thy staff. We thank thee that we are made to be dependent, that none of us can live to himself. But most of all we thank thee that thou art dependable, naming us one by one, marking our several needs, and supplying all that we require, and more, out of the treasure stores of eternal mercy. Hear us, O God, as our hearts at their best, and at their humblest, ascribe unto thee the glory that belongeth to thy name. Thus in praise of thee we find our steadfast, unfrightened hope in thee. . . .

JAMES A. JONES (1911–1966)

From *Prayers for the People* (Richmond: John Knox Press, 1967), 117. © M. E. Bratcher 1967. Used by permission of Westminster John Knox Press.

A Prayer of Waiting

Lord Jesus, You want honest words on my lips: no thought of mine is hidden from You anyway . . . but Lord, why does Your providence have to move so slowly?

I know that the seasons come and go in majestic sequence. The earth rotates on its axis in a predetermined rhythm. No prayers of mine could change any of this. I know that Your ways are not my ways; Your timing is not my timing. But Lord, how do I, so earthbound, come to terms with the pace of eternity?

I want to be teachable, Lord. Is there something You want to show me, some block You want removed, some change You want in me or my attitudes before You can answer my prayer? Give me the gift of eyes that see, of ears that hear what You are saying to me.

Come Lord Jesus, and abide in my heart. How grateful I am to realize that the answer to my prayer does not depend on me at all. As I quietly abide in You and let Your life flow into me, what freedom it is to know that the Father does not see my threadbare patience or insufficient trust, rather only Your patience, and Your confidence that the Father has everything in hand. In Your faith I thank You right now for a more glorious answer to my prayer than I can imagine.

CATHERINE MARSHALL (1914–1984)

Prayer of an African Christian

O God:
Enlarge my heart
   that it may be big enough to receive the greatness of your love.
Stretch my heart
   that it may take into it all those who with me around the world believe in Jesus Christ.
Stretch it
   that it may take into it all those who do not know him, but who are
   my responsibility because I know him.
And stretch it
   that it may take in all those who are not lovely in my eyes, and
   whose hands I do not want to touch;
through Jesus Christ, my Savior. Amen.

KAPINGA ESETÊ (d. 1975)
From Presbyterian Church (U.S.A.), *Walking with Africans*, 23. Translated by Mary B. Crawford. Used by
   permission.

ᴓ Into the Twenty-first Century

At the end of the twentieth century it is possible to look into the new century that is already beginning to take shape. Themes that have been present throughout the ages of the Reformed tradition are still with us: God is still seen as sovereign; the Bible is taken seriously as the seedbed for faith; Christ is central to faith and the One who holds together all the scattered threads of life; confession is still practiced, although with a greater sense of the corporateness of sin.

In addition to these ageless themes, new ones have emerged in the last half of the twentieth century that will continue to influence the life and piety of Reformed Churches in the year 2000 and beyond.

That is one reason we chose to divide later prayers into two chapters, one on twentieth-century prayers and this one that looks to the future. Fifteen of the authors in this chapter are women, several are from the Third World, others are from traditions other than Euro-American within the United States. The issues addressed in these prayers include human liberation from all forms of oppression, including gay liberation and the liberation of women as well as liberation from military governments. These prayers celebrate diversity in a way only pointed to in the first half of the century. What makes them all Reformed? The answer is not easy beyond saying that these authors are members of different Reformed denominations, who are all Christians and make no apology about that. The prayers touch on biblical themes of human worth, the importance of taking creation seriously, the dignity of work, and the importance of peace. They are all christological, and it is commitment to Jesus Christ that holds them together.

The names of these authors are given without dates except for the first author, who is notable because of her age. Whamok Kim Lee, born in 1898, was a Korean evangelist and one of the first women to become a well-known leader in the Presbyterian Church of that country. Geneviève Graves is a professor of dramatic arts who became a Protestant and is a member of a Protestant religious community. Lesslie Newbigin is a Scottish Presbyterian who helped form the United Church of South India and became a bishop in that church. Ernest T. Campbell has served as one of America's greatest preachers and as a voice for justice as pastor of Riverside Church of New York City. Sara Little, a Christian educator, became a pioneering seminary professor when women on seminary faculties were a rarity. Michel Bouttier, a retired professor of New Testament, was a pastor who wrote about his ministry with compassion and genuine spirituality. Benjamin M. Weir was the subject of great national attention during his captivity in the Middle East and has since his release been a voice for reason in the ongoing crisis in that part of the world. Jane Parker Huber is best known as a writer of hymns that have been included in the hymnals of several different denominations. Her hymns often use new images for God. Flora Slosson Wuellner, a pastor in the United Church of Christ, is known and loved for her influence on seminary students and on the wider church because of her many books on the spiritual life. Julia Esquivel is a Guatemalan who has dedicated her life to peace and justice and has paid a high price for her faithfulness. Kálmán Csiha, a Reformed bishop who lives in Romania, is president of the world synod of the Hungarian Reformed Churches. Sara Bernice Moseley, an active Presbyterian elder in Sherman, Texas, was the first woman to serve as moderator of the General Assembly of the Presbyterian Church in the United States. She has long been a tireless worker for Presbyterian Church unity.

Clinton Marsh was moderator of the General Assembly of the United Presbyterian Church in the U.S.A. and has been a prominent African American leader in education as president of Knoxville College. Another important African American Presbyterian is James Costen, who has been the President of the Interdenominational Theological Center in Atlanta and was the last moderator of the General Assembly of the United Presbyterian Church, leading it into reunion. James Andrews served as Stated Clerk of the Presbyterian Church in the United States until reunion and was then elected as the first Stated Clerk for the General Assembly of the Presbyterian Church (U.S.A.). Cecil Corbett is a leading spokesperson for Native Americans within the Presbyterian Church. He served as the first Native American president of Cook School in Tempe, Arizona. Jorge Lara-Braud is an interpreter of Latin American liberation theology within the North American context, having taught at both Austin and San Francisco seminaries.

Joy Patterson is a Presbyterian elder whose hymns have been included in eight contemporary hymnals. Melva W. Costen is an African American educator and musician who was chair of the committee that produced *The Presbyterian Hymnal*. Ann Weems is a poet and writer of creative worship materials. J. Barrie Shepherd is pastor of the First Presbyterian Church in the city of New York and author of books on the Psalms and on prayer. Pavel Filipi is a minister of the Evangelical Church of Czech Brethren.

Joanna Adams is pastor of Trinity Presbyterian Church of Atlanta, Georgia, one of the largest congregations in the denomination to have a woman senior pastor. James P. K. Shum, who was born in China, now serves as pastor of the Chinese Presbyterian Church of Oakland, California.

Greer Anne Wenh-In Ng is a Chinese immigrant to Canada who presently teaches at Emmanuel College, Toronto. Rubem Alves, a Brazilian Presbyterian, was an early voice for liberation theology in Latin America. John de Gruchy is one of the leading Reformed theologians of South Africa. Ruth C. Duck is a pastor in the United Church of Christ and teaches at Garrett-Evangelical Seminary. Daniel Beteta is a Guatemalan by birth and is presently a pastor in Southern California.

Ophelia Manney is the first African American woman to be ordained as a Presbyterian minister in the western United States. Kikanza Nuri Robins is an African American businesswoman and a theology student. Chris Glaser, a leader in the gay and lesbian community within the Presbyterian Church, is a prophetic voice for the unity of justice and prayer. Maake J. Masango is a minister of the Presbyterian Church of Southern Africa and was elected as its moderator in 1996. Patricia Baxter is also a minister of the Presbyterian Church of Southern Africa and an educator. Lutumba Tukadi-Kuetu is a minister in the Reformed Presbyterian Church, of the Democratic Republic of Congo. Elsa Tamez is a Mexican biblical scholar and theologian at the Latin American Biblical Seminary in San José, Costa Rica, of which she is now president.

It is impossible to do complete justice to the wide range of persons and pieties within the Reformed tradition. Every effort will omit some who might have been included. These authors are a cross section of the diversity of the Reformed tradition at this time. They show the inclusivity of a tradition that is following the maxim "The church reformed, but always being reformed." Clearly, God is not done with us yet. Our full international diversity will be demonstrated even more in the next century.

Prayer of Petition
for Those Suffering Persecution

Dear loving Hananim Aboji (God Father), the Alpha and Omega of history and of each of us. You are the creator of all that is on earth and You are Lord of the nations. We, the Korean people, find ourselves under the yoke of a cruel oppressor. We are told in the scriptures that Your chosen children of Israel toiled for generations in the land of Pharaoh. We too cry out, "How long, O Lord, how long?" must we suffer in bondage before we are set free from the horror of colonial rule?

The pain and anguish of our people are great, O God of Moses and Father of the Prince of Peace. It is difficult to see our men humiliated, our women violated, our children brainwashed, our language forbidden, and our culture stripped away. Even so, we will not hate our taskmasters. You have commanded us in Your word to love our enemies in the name and for the sake of Jesus Christ. This we do because of what Jesus did for us on the cross of Calvary and who He is as a living presence by the power of the Holy Spirit in our daily lives. Therefore, we say with him, "Father, forgive them, for they know not what they do."

We pray especially for our families. We are grateful for the fact that even though our beloved peninsula no longer belongs to us, at least our homes remain a sanctuary where we can be true to our country and to ourselves. So it is in the spirit of our ancestors and those brave martyrs who have only recently been put to death because of their refusal to bow down before the Shinto shrine as decreed by our overseers, that we pray and take heart. We thank you for grandfathers and grandmothers, parents and siblings, aunts and uncles, cousins and clans, because it is through these precious ties that bind us together that we experience Your love and care for us.

In gratitude and humility, we await the day of jubilee. Liberation will come to our homeland even though it may take years, decades or even centuries. But come it will, as surely as the East

Sea flows and the mountain winds blow. We may not know what the future holds but we know that You hold the future. Most of all, we thank You for Jesus Christ, the same yesterday, today, and forever. In the name of this King of Kings and Lord of Lords we pray. Amen.

WHAMOK KIM LEE (b. 1898)
Translated by her son, Warren W. Lee, and used by permission.

To Love Those Whom I Do Not Love

Lord,
You who love this person whom I do not love,
you who read the hearts of others whom I do not understand,
you who know the inmost suffering of those whom I ignore,
you who discern the efforts of each one in attitudes which I
perceive as deceitful:
   open my eyes and my heart.
You also know me far better than I know myself;
   you love me better than I love myself. . . .
Lord! Teach me to love with your love.

GENEVIÈVE GRAVES
In Chapal and Pellegrin, *La tradition calvinienne*, 81. © Editions C.L.D. 1981. Used by permission.

For the Unity of the Church

Grant, O Lord God, that thy church, as it hath one foundation and one head, may verily and indeed be one body; holding forth one faith, proclaiming one truth, and following one Lord in holiness of living and love, even thy Son our Saviour, Jesus Christ. Amen.

LESSLIE NEWBIGIN
From World Student Christian Federation, *Venite Adoremus II*, 185. Used by permission of the World Student Christian Federation, Geneva.

Preparation for the Lord's Supper

Most gracious God, as thou hast called us to this thy table, give us grace, we beseech thee, in this hour so to hear thy word and so to let thy Spirit search our hearts that we may come prepared in faith and penitence and joy to receive the gift of the body and blood of Jesus Christ, thy Son our Lord.

LESSLIE NEWBIGIN

From World Student Christian Federation, *Venite Adoremus II*, 208. Used by permission of the World Student Christian Federation, Geneva.

For Lent

As we near the hallowed grounds of Gethsemane and Golgotha, we confess to a sense of unworthiness and shame.
> Our deprivations are so few,
> Our scars so scarce,
> Our courage so seldom summoned,
> Our passion so wasted on self.
Who are we that we should bear thy name or purport to be thy people?

Forgive us, O God, for we know not what we do.
> Expose the games we play with thee to stave off the moment of full surrender; and help us to come as the sinners we are, that we may obtain mercy and find help in time of need.
Our prayers we offer in faith and with thanksgiving,
> through Jesus Christ our Lord. Amen.

ERNEST T. CAMPBELL

From Leo S. Thorne, ed., *Prayers from Riverside*, 40. Copyright © 1983 The Pilgrim Press. Used by permission of the publisher.

At Commencement

We praise Thee, O God, for this day, which is both an ending and a beginning.

Thou hast forgiven us and healed us and brought us from different backgrounds, communities, and denominations, to this moment. Now past and present merge into the future—a future we face with hope, because Thou art a living God. But it is also a future we face with uncertain courage, knowing our own weaknesses, and failures, and doubts, and inability to do even the truth we know.

Make us willing to be earthen vessels, not demanding perfection of ourselves, yet willing to be transformed by that treasure, to which we witness, given by Thee. And thus may we continue in our ministry with joy and confidence, knowing our fellowship with that great company of saints to which, by thy grace, we belong.

In Christ's name. Amen.

SARA LITTLE
Used by permission of the author.

On the First Day of a Course

We thank you, O God, that we are together in this time and place, aware of your presence and grateful for the fellowship that we have with one another because of your love for us. May we be open to one another, and to hearing and responding to You. And now we commit unto you the work of this course, praying that what we do shall be done to your name's honor and glory. Amen.

SARA LITTLE (1995)
Used by permission of the author.

Prayer of Return

Your presence, Lord,
is sometimes peaceful and happy
because it is expected, welcomed, adored.
There is also this bitter and tenacious presence
by which You pursue me
when I will not give myself to You.

I have fled from You, Lord,
and yet I have not been at peace for one instant
during all these weeks: Your gaze has been
constantly fixed on me, Your sad gaze.
O grant me, Lord, to know You now
in Your power and Your joy!

MICHEL BOUTTIER

From Michel Bouttier, *Prayers for My Village*, translated by Lamar Williamson, 70. Copyright © 1994 Upper Room Books. Used by permission of the publisher.

Emmaus

Lord, we had walked a long time without being able to recognize You. We were going along together, but our hearts were heavy, heavy with defeat, with hurt feelings, with fogginess, and with indifference. We were saying as we walked that it's all over for our people here and the stone of the tomb has rolled shut on all our hopes.

Then, this Sunday, You gathered us around the table.
The bread was broken, our eyes were opened,
and we recognized You . . .
this great fraternal circle, so often torn,
Your resurrected body!

MICHEL BOUTTIER ·
From Michel Bouttier, *Prayers for My Village*, translated by Lamar Williamson, 67. Copyright © 1994 Upper Room Books. Used by permission of the publisher.

Prayer of a Captive

Lord, I remember your promise, and I think it applies to me too. I've done nothing to deserve it but receive it as a free gift. I'm in need. I need you. I need your assurance and guidance to be faithful to you in this situation. Teach me what I need to learn. Deliver me from this place and this captivity if it is your will. If it is not your will to set me free, help me to accept whatever is involved. Show me your gifts and enable me to recognize them as coming from you. Thank you for your encouraging presence. Praise be to you.

BENJAMIN WEIR
From *Hostage Bound, Hostage Free*, 31. © 1987 Ben and Carol Weir. Used by permission of Westminster John Knox Press.

Prayer for Peace

Great God, whose will is peace for all the earth
Sung forth in joy at Christ our Savior's birth,
Now we too sing the news with sparkling mirth.

Turn us around to paths of love and peace,
Reshape our minds that petty strife may cease.
And songs will soar and harmony increase.

Destroy our trust in weapon, bomb, and sword,
Renew our faith in tools of true accord.
Call us again to Christ, our living Lord.

Peacemakers! Blessed by Christ's inviting word,
Children of God, let everywhere be heard
The sounds of peace and justice not deferred.

Almighty One, your way is our shalom.
Trusting your light, we pilgrim people roam.
Bring us, at last, to our eternal home.

JANE PARKER HUBER

From *A Singing Faith*, no. 56. © 1987 Jane Parker Huber. Used by permission of Westminster John Knox Press.

Prayer of the Rope's End

Living Christ, I know you are with me. This situation is more than I can handle. I am in over my head. I give you this whole problem now. Take it over, the whole thing, all the way. Fill me, fill this place, fill all of us who are here with your transforming presence. I thank you that at this moment you are enfolding us. In your name, by your word, and through your power. Amen.

FLORA SLOSSON WUELLNER
Author's adaptation from *Prayer, Fear, and Our Powers* (Nashville: Upper Room Books), 95. Copyright © 1989 Flora Slosson Wuellner. Used by permission.

Family

Where are your brothers
and your mother, Lord,
Your family?
Freedom, achingly rich,
beyond comprehension:
To be alone
when your sword runs us through
driving us mad
with the madness of your compassion
and you lift us up,
mothers, brothers and sisters,
in all those who, having no place
to lay their heads,
make up your family.

Alone before You,
I found mother,
brother,
comrade,

son,
husband,
perfect stature.
Word of mercy, clothed with my flesh,
sustained with my bones,
incarnate in all the crucified
of History.

Your family,
numerous as the sands of the sea,
luminous as the stars in the sky.

My family, your little brothers,
heirs of your Kingdom,
Revive in me the flame
of your love.

JULIA ESQUIVEL. Written in the early morning of July 26, 1991, the day Aunt Ceci received
the Lord's embrace at five in the afternoon.
In *Gifts from Latin Americans*, 31. © Presbyterian Church (U.S.A.), 1996. Used by permission of the author.

Song from the Deep

Christ our Lord, Your orphaned nation
Looks to You from prison's darkness.
Our hearts burn in Your creation,
By Your mercy make our pain less!

Let Your Holy Spirit's bright flame
Permeate our pain-racked heart.
Let your blood assuage the blame,
And for our sighs your peace impart.

Our prison, like the depths of a crypt
Buries us 'neath this world in fire.
Oh, descend to the depths of the crypt;
Let not Your children there expire!

Teach us how to bear our hardship,
Give us strength to go on chanting,
Convert us under Your hard whip
When pain befalls us without ending.

Let Your Holy Spirit's bright flame
Permeate our pain-racked heart.
Let your blood assuage the blame,
And for our sighs your peace impart.

BISHOP KÁLMÁN CSIHA

From Kálmán Csiha, *Light through the Bars*, trans. Stephen Szabo (Richmond Heights, Ohio: "The Light"
    Publication Project, [1996]), 14 (adapted). Used by permission.

Prayer for the New Church

God of history—
We give you thanks for the line of pilgrims who have worshiped you and have sought to serve you.

>We thank you for the faithful preservation of all kinds of persons in the history of the church that has brought us to this time of celebration and challenge.

>We thank you that in times of stumbling and error you have continued to be with the church as it moves toward new beginnings. Most of all, we thank you that your love has come to this world in the life, death, and resurrection of Jesus Christ.

Oh God, your steadfast love stands always ready to forgive, to correct, to uphold us. We confess that even as we give thanks and celebrate, our praise is still somewhat off-key:

>We speak of "our" church. . . .

>We say that "they" do things so differently. . . .

>We still cling to our old comfortable ways. . . .

>We ourselves want to define what "success" can mean in the new church. . . .

>Remind us over and over *whose* church this is and who is its Head.

God of the future—

>We bring before you our dreams and visions and hopes for this new church.

>Tie these dreams into the very heart of this needy world.

Help us to stand with all Christians as we seek together to be your agents of reconciliation. For it is in your providence that the birth pangs of this new church may result in new strength of witness, and it is to your glory that the body of Christ shall be built up.

These prayers we bring in the name of Christ, great Head of the Church. Amen.

SARA BERNICE MOSELEY. From "Our Pilgrimage Toward Reunion," a celebration of Presbyterian heritage on August 13, 1983, at Montreat, North Carolina. Sara Moseley had chaired the Presbyterian Church, U.S., Friends for Reunion.
Used by permission of the author.

Petition for Grace

Listen, God, you who said you would hear a sinner's prayer.

We come, this morning, truly as sinners—each and every one, and all of us as sinners together.

We come as true children of Adam and Eve, deciding that we, too, will do things our way. And doing things our way we come with lives twisted and warped. We see what we've done to ourselves and we abhor it. Yet we must come to you just as we are. So, Lord, we come seeking unity, mercy, while mercy may be found.

With our relation with you broken, we are alienated within ourselves. We, who should love ourselves with a healthy love, detest ourselves and are sick inwardly.

Detesting ourselves, we cannot truly love our fellow human beings, so we live in wretched human relations.

We throw ourselves on your grace, seeking your forgiveness. In your forgiving, enable us to have peace with ourselves. With inner peace, may we have reconciliation with our human associates.

Truly, Lord, may we find mercy while mercy is to be found.

And may we live in such ways that others may see Christ in us and seek to know the joys of fellowship with him.

This prayer comes from the depths of our hearts in the name of Jesus. Amen and amen.

CLINTON MARSH
Used by permission of the author.

Prayer on the Occasion of the
Atlanta Visit of Nelson Mandela

Almighty God, in the midst of this and every chaos you always manage to raise up people and circumstances to bridge the gap and bring hope out of despair. It has been said, "You may not come when we want you, but you are always on time."

We remember how when Israel was captive in Egypt, you raised up MOSES to start their journey toward freedom in Canaan.

We recall with joy how you caused an emaciated MOHANDAS to gain the strength of body and mind to free the people of India.

MALCOLM also comes to mind. From a background of poverty you enabled him to possess the disciplines of mind and character to inspire millions to higher heights of dignity and self-worth.

Then, Lord, there was MARTIN. Generations presently living, and those yet to be born, cannot thank him enough for the dedication, determination, wisdom, and vision of his leadership. He rescued a nation whose sense of morality was skewed by racism and exclusion.

And now, Lord, you send MANDELA, how timely, how needed. What can we say except "thank you." For almost three decades his imprisonment in South Africa, while threatening to his body, did nothing but increase his resolve that freedom must come to an apartheid-ridden people. And now he is free. With the single-mindedness of the prophets of old he is saying to kings, presidents, and popes, "Let freedom roll down like the mighty waters." Apartheid in South Africa must be enabled to become a never again used relic of history.

His desire, Lord, is the same as your desire. You did not use your creative mind to bring into being first- and second-class citizens. For this, God of all life, we are grateful, and we will use that portion of life still available to us to be faithful to you and to the cause of freedom.

Hear our prayer, O Lord, and grant us the courage to do that for which we pray. Keep Nelson Mandela safe and productive, and we shall give you the honor and the praise today and forevermore.

Amen!

JAMES COSTEN. Offered at Atlanta University Center Convocation, June 27, 1990.
Used by permission of the author.

Petition for a
Sense of Humor about Ourselves

Most gracious God,
　　There are times when we hope you have the capacity to laugh at us,
　　　　because the situations in which we as people involve ourselves
　　　　　　must be taken with a grain of humor,
　　　　　　　　else all is really a tragedy.
Help us also to laugh at ourselves as you laugh at us;
　　to realize that we are not permanent monuments to your gospel,
　　　　that we are temporary servants in the temple.
Give us an understanding of the mysteries that will sustain us
　　so that we can advise those others who come seeking your will.
And never let us think that we have final answers.
　　In Jesus' name.
　　Amen.

JAMES E. ANDREWS

From James E. Andrews, *Prayers for All Seasons*, edited by Vic Jameson, 80. Used by permission of the
　author.

Gratitude for Creation

Creator God, your presence is as the wind, the breath and sustainer of life. We are grateful for being a part of your beautiful creation; rugged mountains, rolling plains, and uncultivated desert. We thank you for the birds of the air, animals, and fish of the sea. For purity of water and air and healing medicines that remind us of the need for holy virtue in life, physical and spiritual.

In your holy mystery, you have revealed that we are God's children, a wonderful mosaic of humanity with different cultures and heritages. We have a work yet to do, to work for truth and equity. We pray that we might always be found faithful, reflecting your love.

Cause light to overcome the darkness in this world. Be present, O God, through your Son Jesus, in whose name we pray.

CECIL CORBETT (Nez Percé)
Used by permission of the author.

Help Me Today
to Serve the World Well

Gracious God, perhaps I should quit this habit of reading two newspapers before I go to work. The world I read about seems to get worse each day. It's enough to make me throw in the towel and to leave it to the rascals to finish it off.

But then, I remember it is *this* world you love, not another, and I begin to re-focus. There is hope for the world and for me, after all. Your love is at work, even in the midst of violence and death. I know it because your dear child Jesus was not overcome by either violence or death, but overcame them both by the power of your love. That's all I need to know.

Help me, then, not to flinch away from the daily news, to serve the world truly well, and to do it with all the gifts you have given me, the greatest of which is love. Amen.

JORGE LARA-BRAUD
Used by permission of the author.

Prayer for the City

O Lord, You gave Your servant John
A vision of the world to come:
A radiant city filled with light,
Where You with us will make Your home;
Where neither grief nor pain shall dwell,
Since former things have passed away,
And where they need no sun nor moon;
Your glory lights eternal day.

Our cities, Lord, wear shrouds of pain;
Beneath our gleaming towers of wealth
The homeless crouch in rain and snow,
The poor cry out for strength and health.
Youth's hope is dimmed by ignorance;
Unwilling, workers idled stand;
Indifference walks unheeding by
As hunger stretches out its hand.

Come, Lord, make real John's vision fair;
Come, dwell with us, make all things new;
We try in vain to save our world
Unless our help shall come from You.
Come, strengthen us to live in love;
Bid hatred, greed, injustice cease.
Your glory all the light we need,
Let all our cities shine forth peace.

JOY F. PATTERSON

The Classic
African American Folk Prayer

Almighty! and all wise God our heavenly father! 'tis once more and again that a few of your beloved children are gathered together to call upon your holy name. We bow at your footstool of mercy, Master, to thank you for our spared lives. We thank you that we are able to get up this morning clothed in our right mind, for Master, since we met here, many have been snatched out of the land of the living and hurled into eternity. But through your goodness and mercy we have been spared to assemble ourselves here once more to call upon a Captain who has never lost a battle. Oh, throw round us your strong arms of protection. Bind us together in love and union. Build us up where we are torn down and strengthen us where we are weak. Oh, Lord! Oh Lord! take the lead of our minds, place them on heaven and heavenly divine things. Oh, God, our Captain and our King! Search our hearts, Master, as far as the east is from the west. Now Lord you know our hearts, you know our heart's desire. You know our down-setting and our up-rising. Lord you know all about us 'cause you made us. Lord! Lord! One more kind favor I ask you. Remember the man that is to stand in the gateway and proclaim your Holy Word. Oh, stand by him. Strengthen him where he is weak and build him up where he is torn down. Oh, let him down into the deep treasures of your word.

And now, oh, Lord, when this humble servant is done down here in this low land of sorrow; done sitting down and getting up; done being called everything but a child of God; oh, when I am done, done, done, and this old world can afford me no longer, right soon in the morning, Lord, right soon in the morning, meet me down at the river of Jordan, bid the water to be still, tuck my little soul away in that low swinging chariot, and bear it away over yonder in the third heaven where every day will be Sunday and my sorrows of this old world will have an end, is my prayer for Christ's my Redeemer's sake and amen and thank God.

MELVA W. COSTEN. This is Professor Costen's recollection of the folk prayer that she heard in the black Presbyterian Church of her youth. Versions of it were still being heard in the 1980s and 1990s in African American churches of various denominations.
In J. M. Washington, *Conversations with God: Two Centuries of Prayers by African Americans* (New York: HarperCollins, 1994), 245.

Lament Psalm Twenty-four

O my God, it is not fair!
I watch other people
come and go.
They walk and talk
and eat and play.
They laugh; they travel; they work;
they marry and give birth,
but we sit around the table of death.
We do not smile, nor do we live.
We are suspended in that one moment,
that one moment of death.
When his life was taken,
our lives were forever changed.
O our God, why aren't you fair to us?
Why were we the ones chosen
to weep?

It is not fair, O God!
Everybody knows we belong to you.
We declared it in the sanctuary.
Why, O God of mercy,
do we sit at the table of death?
Move us, O God of power; move us
to the table of life!
Give us bread and give us wine
in the name of your son
let us live again!
If you would just
break the bread of life
over our heads,
the crumbs would be sufficient.

If you would just pour the wine
close to us,
the splash would revive us.

O God of glory,
our dead hearts beat again.
The hosannas rush out of our mouths,
and we bow down
in the presence of our God
who is life eternal.

ANN WEEMS
From *Psalms of Lament*, 43–44. © 1995 Ann B. Weems. Used by permission of Westminster John Knox Press.

With Me, Lord

Before I awaken this morning
you are with me, Lord,
and even as I open my eyes
you greet me with the gift of this new day.
May I take this certainty of your presence
with me into all this day can hold.
Be with me now as I go forth—
not as some weird
and ghostly watcher-over-me,
but as a deeper and truer awareness within:
an awareness
which is constantly
opening my heart to trust,
to hope,
to sharing and giving,
to the call of the needs
of my fellow-creatures;
an awareness
which is constantly
opening all of my senses
to the hidden joys,
the tiny discoveries,
the lesser celebrations
and the over-arching wonder
of your gift of life.

J. BARRIE SHEPHERD

Prayer of Intercession

Heavenly Father,
your Son gave us the right to call to you in His name.
We make use of this right now and intercede
   —for those who have lost trust in your word and do not believe that
      you are governing your creation;
   —for those who do not see your bright face because of their sin;
   —for those whose lives are growing dark because of illness, care of
      fellow people, betrayal or injustice which they have suffered;
   —for all hungry, suffering, persecuted and abandoned ones, and
      also for all those who struggle against hunger, misery, injus-
      tice, diseases and war;
   —for your church. May it be a clear sign of the new order in your
      kingdom.
   —for those who administer public affairs and bear responsibility for
      peace and justice in the world.
Be merciful to all of us.
Our Father . . . (the Lord's Prayer)
Amen.

PAVEL FILIPI
Translated by Martin Prudký from Evangelical Church of Czech Brethren, *Sbírka kázání* (Sermon collection) (Prague, 1993), 245. Used by permission.

A Morning Prayer

Grant to me, if it be your pleasure:
—spontaneity and discipline, laughter and reverence, energy and
    rest;
—the patience to take each day an hour at a time and the wisdom to
    handle whatever happens with common sense and trust in
    your everlasting love and unfailing grace.
May my spirit be free from
—fear and irritability
—self-doubt and dark clouds.
May I be a window through whom the light of life shines, and may I
be ever mindful of the good I know, as well as of the needs of others.
Through Christ my Lord. Amen.

JOANNA M. ADAMS (1997)
Used by permission of the author.

Thanksgiving
for Cultural Diversity

Dear God, Creator of the universe, maker of all nations; we bow before you for your mighty wisdom which we experience in our lives. Every nation has its customs and culture which reflect the diversity and unity of your greatness. We are different in style, custom, shape, size, and language, yet we are one. We are one humanity under your tender care because you are love. You embrace us with your arms and nurture us with your spirit. We cultivate and create our culture and customs. Your love helps us to see in depth that all cultures of this universe reveal some part of your nature. The only way to understand you clearly is through Jesus Christ our Lord.

We thank you, Lord, for your Spirit inspires us to receive Jesus as Lord so that when we celebrate our Chinese New Year and other festivals, we can proclaim that you are the God who celebrates with us for your name's sake. Help us to keep the spirit and the virtue of our heritage and give thanks to you. We thank you for our seniors who share stories with us. We thank you for those people who work hard to keep the spirit of the New Year within our lives. We appreciate the experience of the communion of saints so that in the four seas we are brothers and sisters. Lord of love and forgiveness, lead us and guide us all the way, wherever we go and whatever we do. Amen.

JAMES P. K. SHUM

Great Prayer of Thanksgiving
from a Multicultural Perspective

It is indeed good and right to give you thanks and praise,
God of many names. You made a covenant with Noah,
and caused nations, in their amazing diversity
of culture, ethnicity and language,
to spread over the face of the earth.
As of old you led your people
out of a land of enslavement to a land of promise,
so too you led our ancestors and some of us
into new lands of possibility, there to find you anew.

In the fullness of time you sent Jesus,
in every aspect human as we are,
to grow up in a small town in Galilee
speaking with a distinct accent,
far from the seat of religious and civil power.
In his ministry he was challenged by a gentile mother
to re-think his stance into inclusivity;
Beside Jacob's well he was moved
by an encounter with a minority woman
to disclose his messianic identity.

On the last night he spent with his friends,
Jesus took an age-old tradition from his people
and transformed it into something new.
He took bread, the staple food of his land,
blessed and broke it, and gave it to those around him,
saying, "Take, eat, this is my body, broken for you.
Whenever you do this, remember me."
After supper he took a cup of wine,
common drink of his people, and gave it to them,

saying, "Drink this, all of you,
This is the new covenant in my blood;
Each time you do this, remember me."

(The following may be added when using alternative Asian elements)

So now we take this cake, made from rice,
the precious daily food of many on this earth,
rice grown in wet paddy fields in tropical climes;
and we take tea, daily drink of many everywhere,
from leaves gathered by sisters on distant hillsides,
to share among us as we remember
our Lord and Savior, Jesus, the Christ.

GREER ANNE WENH-IN NG
Used by permission of the author.

A Prayer for Deliverance

You know, O God,
how hard it is to survive captivity without any hope of the Holy City.
Sing to us, God, the songs of the promised land.
Serve us your manna in the desert,
and give us grace to enjoy our day of rest
as an expression of our trust.

Let there be, in some place,
a community of men, women, elderly, children, and new-born babies
as a first fruit, as our appetizer,
and an embrace of the future. Amen.

RUBEM A. ALVES
In John Carden, *With All God's People*, 126. Geneva: WCC Publications, 1989. Used by permission.

Lord, Teach Us to Love

It is easy, Lord, to mouth the word,
to say "I love," but not to practice what it means.
When we see the true love of a lover,
the extent to which such love is prepared to go for the beloved,
to vault over mountains and dive under waves, we know our love is
paltry, self-seeking, a denial of the word.
When we consider your love,
the love of the cross,
the descent into the depths of hell in search of us,
your forgiveness which overwhelms and heals us,
we know our love is cheap, our forgiveness empty,
judgmental and graceless.
Teach us to love you with heart, soul and mind,
to love our neighbour and our enemy.
Teach us to forgive as you have forgiven us.

JOHN DE GRUCHY

From John de Gruchy, *Cry Justice: Prayers, Meditations, and Readings from South Africa* (Maryknoll, N.Y.: Orbis Books, 1986), 219. Used by permission of HarperCollins Publishers Ltd., London.

For the New Year

Now that the mad rush is over,
O center of stillness and peace;
Now that the needles are falling from the tree,
We thank you that you are still God-with-us.
As we face the year ahead,
help us to accept the difficult parts of our lives;
help us to make the changes we must make;
bring us to new places of openness and love toward you
    and the people around us;
help us to overcome the fears which keep us from fullness of life.
As the frigid days of January and February draw near
Help us to keep warm places alive within us,
where in secret
in the bulbs of springtime tulips are nurtured.
As we face the year ahead,
we thank you for one another
and for your grace in Jesus Christ.
Help us individually and as a congregation
to be signs of your compassion,
hope, joy, and unity
in this world you love in Jesus
our Christ, Amen.

RUTH C. DUCK

Prayer for the Land

The earth is no longer producing fruit,
it has become sterile.
God, You have always been just;
I am not abandoned.
In Your hands, loving God,
You have caused prosperity to blossom;
do not leave me forsaken now,
for I am your needy son.

My lands and my plow
need your blessing,
my sons and my nation
implore your care.

God as always powerful,
come and bloom in our land;
fill us with generous corn
to prosper our crop.

May the early rain
come in its time and make earth fruitful.
Bless us in the same way
and may your Spirit purify us.
Amen.

DANIEL BETETA
Translated by Daniel Beteta, Jr. Used by permission.

Jesus, Christmas Is Your Birthday

Jesus, long ago, at Mother's house, I did not see you walking or talking.
Christmas was turkey, large and golden brown—brothers and sisters,
    laughing with few frowns.
Jesus, you were there, but where?
Were you in the giant white and blue bulbed tree?
Were you there for me?
I wandered around that roomy house,
    where you were to be found.
Jesus this is your day, show us the way.
Did we all find you, a loving heart, sent from God,
    being sent as a Son, like a big tall brother who gave his life for another.
Jesus, Christmas is your day that you gave us forever.
I saw you long ago under a moonlit night.
The sky was aglow from my uncurtained window.
Did mother see you? I hope that father did too.
He always said, "It's all about love."
Thank you that he is now above in your kingdom
No need to explain Christmas in that celestial place,
    laced with love and grace.
Thank you for another Christmas day.

OPHELIA MANNEY
Used by permission of the author.

A Prayer for Intervention

Mother God, without you I know I am not. Today I am feeling that even with you, I am not very much. As I pray, I know I am surrounded and protected by your light. I clear my mind of troubled thoughts. Pushing them aside for this moment, I create a path for you to come and sit with me. I feel your arm around my shoulders. I feel your hand stroking my forehead. I hear your voice reminding me gently that you are here with me and your goodness is a part of me. I breathe in the pure air that is your wake, and it purifies my thoughts. With the light from your eyes, I discern truth from the false evidence that looks so real today. I surrender my ego, my pride, and my arrogant independence to the truth and love that surround and embrace me now. I open my hands to receive the bounties that are before me, even though I can't see them today. And I give thanks. Amen.

KIKANZA NURI ROBINS

Prayer for Those with AIDS

Dear God,
friends with AIDS
slip through my fingers
faster than grains of sand,
and seemingly, as many.

I can't hold them.

God, dear God,
please catch them
with your open hands,
within your welcoming embrace,
and with your loving heart.

I wish I could be there for them.

I pray they'll be there for me
when I slip.
You are my God,
our God.
Amen.

CHRIS GLASER. Dedicated to the memory of Lyle Loder.
From *Coming Out to God*, 129. © 1991 Chris R. Glaser. Used by permission of Westminster John Knox Press.

Prayer for Africa

The sun that is so good,
Messiah, the one who warms us with God's love. A God who is a
friend of
   African
   Asian
   American
   and all God's people;
We come to you as children in need of your love.
We come because you are God, full of love.
Gracious God, you are the creator of us all,
Help us to adore and worship you in spirit and in truth.
You are a friend to those who are broken,
   a parent to those who are orphans.
You are a God of love, peace and mercy.
We come to you because you are a fountain and a source of love.
Help us to love and care for each other, especially those who are poor.
Help us to care for each other so that all the barriers that exist between
   rich and poor
   old and young
   angry and gentle
   first world and third world
may be dismantled.
Give to each of us listening hearts in such a way that the pain, hurt and
cries of your people may enable us to respond and move forward following your example, healing them as we heal ourselves. Bind us together, Lord, powerful countries as well as poor countries, that we
may work for peace.
Hear our prayers from the land of Africa, the land full of
   blood
   genocide
   political killings
   instability.

Women are raped in thousands; help us to see your image in them.
Help us, God of love, to hear others.
We pray for the church in Rwanda.
Judge eternal, you know how we compromise and accept standards that are low; help us, fulfilling God, to love as you have loved us. Amen.

MAAKE J. MASANGO
Used by permission of the author.

It's All Very Well
Wanting Liberation

God of Vision,
You have brought women together
to bring their concerns before the Assembly.
Thank you for opening doors for truth to be heard.
Liberation to serve you is indeed a worthy path,
because you tell us that we are made in your likeness:
a woman,
    Godly created, beautiful in your sight. . . .
It's all very well wanting liberation,
    but then the expectations of our world
come crashing onto your sacred vision, saying,
You are only a woman,
    you should not represent me in the sanctuary;
you are only a woman,
    do not expect to be a part of major decisions;
you are only a woman,
    a wonderful provider in the home.
Dare we not face the public
    with views different from a man's?
It's all very well wanting the liberation you promise
    but we are wounded, we need your healing
    to guide us into new paths.
Why do so few hear your invitation to heal women?
Why do so many use your name in vain,
    holding women in poverty and men in bondage
    to male authority?
Bring sapiential authority into our midst, O wise one.

Hear our cry for freedom from culture and doctrines
    that bind us in
worldly limitations.
Hear our cry to be used in your service
    as a witness for others.
Amen.

PATRICIA BAXTER
Used by permission of the author.

Prayer of the Kasai

Mvidi Mukulu, Elder Spirit, Loving Judge,
Brilliant Sun who blinds those looking at You,
The Bounteous Provider who feeds even the animals of the forest,
Father of our ancestors and Father of our Chief, Jesus,
We give You thanks and praise.
　Yesu Kilisto, Jesus Christ, Chief of all Chiefs,
You are the gourd of the water of reconciliation which we drink
to cool our conflict with God, our neighbor, ourselves.
You are the *Tshinkunku* tree around which our hunters gather to con-
　fess sins to each other.
You heal sickness and weakness and sin today even as You did in Israel.
The ancestors said that a son equals his father, thus You are truly God.
　Mueyelu wa Mvidi Mukulu, Breath of God, Holy Spirit,
You are the wind of power moving in and among us cleansing, liber-
　ating, and sustaining.
Through You we become joined to people of every tribe and nation.
It is You who give birth to the Church and cause it to move.
　Our God, we give You thanks and praise for Your mercy to us.
When we came to this land, You were already here. Though we sleep
through the night as if dead, we awaken each morning to life. Give
grace to your Church that we might be the hand of Your salvation, of
Your liberation to the people of all tribes.
In the name of Jesus, Amen.

LUTUMBA TUKADI-KUETU
From Presbyterian Church (U.S.A.), *Walking with Africans*, 20. Translated by Hunter Farrell. Used by per-
　mission.

Invitation to Communion

Leader: Come people, come to the table of the Lord,
              Together we will make a giant loaf
              and together prepare the jars of wine
              as at the wedding feast of Cana.

Community: Come, people, come to the table of the Lord.

Leader: May the woman not forget the salt
              nor the man forget the yeast
              and we shall invite many guests;
              the crippled, the blind, the mute, the poor.

Community: Come, people, come to the table of the Lord.

Leader: And now, we shall follow the Lord's instruction.
              Together we knead the dough with our hands
              and watch how the loaf rises.

Community: Come, people, come to the table of the Lord.

Leader: Because today we're celebrating our promise to Jesus
                 Christ,
              Today we are renewing our promise to the kingdom
              and no one will be hungry.

Community: Come, people, come to the table of the Lord.

ELSA TAMEZ

From *Gifts from Latin Americans: A Celebration of Life*, Mission Interpretation and Promotion, Congregational Ministries Division, Presbyterian Church (U.S.A.). © Presbyterian Church (U.S.A.) [1996]. Used by permission.

ᐊ Contemporary Liturgies

The twentieth century has witnessed a renewed interest in liturgy among Christians in many parts of the world. Reformed churches have been engaged in a process of reconsideration of their own tradition in the light of the ecumenical movement. While they have held to many Reformed liturgical distinctives such as the prayer for right hearing of the Word, they have also borrowed from traditions that have celebrated the seasons of the Christian year. The century has seen the publication of many new service books. There are also instances in which the new service books indicate the development of liturgies appropriate to the particular situations of people at this point in history, such as services for the dissolution of a marriage or services for commissioning people for community service. Both the diversity and the commonality of the tradition of Reformed churches is evident in these prayers. Of course, the limitations of space permit only a few examples to be included here. We have attempted to make selections based on a representation of different denominations and different nations, and on the inclusion of such a variety of prayers that the reader can grasp the liturgical breadth of the tradition. Prayers in this section appear in the order of the date of their publication.

Prayer for the Baptism of Children

Most holy and merciful Father, we give Thee hearty thanks that Thou hast numbered us amongst Thy people, and dost also call our children unto Thee, marking them with this Sacrament, as a singular token and badge of Thy love. Wherefore, we beseech Thee to confirm Thy favour more and more toward us, and to take into Thy tuition and defense *this Child*, whom we offer and present unto Thee with common supplications. Grant that he (she) may know Thee his (her) merciful Father, through Thy Holy Spirit working in his (her) heart, and that he (she) may not be ashamed to confess the faith of Christ crucified; but may continue His faithful soldier and servant, and so prevail against evil that in the end he (she) may obtain the victory, and be exalted into the liberty of Thy kingdom; through Jesus Christ our Lord. Amen.

PRESBYTERIAN CHURCH IN THE U.S.A.
From *The Book of Common Worship* (1906), 41.

Prayer for a Congregation

We thank you for the peace of our country and our homes.
We pray that the fruits of work well done
may give joy to every worker.
Give your blessing to our congregation and church.
May we truly praise you and serve all your people.
We pray for our homeland,
for the leaders of our nation,
and for all who have power and bear responsibility.
We pray for our loved ones,
and for those who have lived and died in the faith.
May we follow their example,
and with them have a share in your kingdom of peace and light.
through our Lord Jesus Christ. Amen.

REFORMED CHURCH IN HUNGARY
From John Carden, ed., *With All God's People* (Geneva: WCC Publications, 1989), 163 (adapted). Used by
permission of the Reformed Church in Hungary.

Prayer for the
Ordination of a Minister

Almighty God and everlasting Father,
who dost govern all things in heaven and earth
by Thy wisdom,
and hast from the beginning
ordained for Thy Church the ministry of reconciliation,
giving some apostles, and some prophets, and some evangelists,
and some pastors and teachers,
for the perfecting of the saints,
for the work of the ministry,
for the edifying of the Body of Christ:

SEND DOWN THY HOLY SPIRIT UPON THIS THY SERVANT, WHOM WE, IN THY NAME AND IN OBEDIENCE TO THY HOLY WILL, DO NOW BY THE LAYING ON OF OUR HANDS ORDAIN AND APPOINT TO THE OFFICE OF THE HOLY MINISTRY IN THY CHURCH, COMMITTING UNTO *him/her* AUTHORITY TO PREACH THE WORD, THE SACRAMENTS, AND TO BEAR RULE IN THY CHURCH.

Bestow upon *him/her* the grace of Thy Holy Spirit,
confirming in heaven what we do in Thy Church on earth,
and owning *him/her* as a true Minister of the Gospel of Thy Son.
Like *his/her* Master, may *he/she* sanctify *himself/herself,*
that others may be sanctified through the truth.
Let the same mind be in *him/her* which was also in Christ Jesus.
May *he/she* quicken and nourish Thy people
in the faith of the Gospel.
Increase *his/her* own faith in Thee, our God.
Abiding in the fellowship of Thy Son,
may *his/her* speech be full of sincerity and truth.
May *he/she* by *his/her* words and works show forth the power of the
    Gospel,
to the saving of people and the glory of Thy holy name.
Grant this, O Heavenly Father,
for the sake of Thy dear Son Jesus Christ;
in whose name we pray.

PRESBYTERIAN CHURCH IN THE U.S.A.
From *The Book of Common Worship* (1946), 228–29 (adapted). Used by permission of Westminster John
    Knox Press.

Prayer of Gratitude

O God, Creator, Redeemer, and Sanctifier,
we thank you that we may be together
to hear your word of life and hope.
We are all equal before you.
You know our life in its deepest recesses.
You have not forgotten us;
    you love us, and again and again you fill the empty hands
    which we stretch out towards you.
Through the suffering and death of your Son Jesus Christ,
you took our darkness and fear upon yourself
in order that we might know light and joy.

PRAYER OF THE WALDENSIAN CHURCH
From John Carden, ed., *With All God's People* (Geneva: WCC Publications, 1989), 317. Used with permission of the Waldensian Church, Rome, and Claudiana Editrice, Turin.

Prayer for Right Hearing
of God's Word

O God, inexhaustible source of all good things, we bless thee
for the gifts of thy love. Grant that we may hear thy word with a
real desire to receive what it promises and to practice what it
commands. Engrave it not only on our minds but in our hearts,
and transform us by thy Spirit into the image of thy Son, making
us contemplate thy glory in the clear mirror of thy gospel.

LITURGY OF THE REFORMED CHURCH OF FRANCE (1963)
From World Student Christian Federation, *Venite Adoremus II*, 33. Used by permission of the World Student Christian Federation, Geneva.

Prayer for the Nation

O God, who art the Ruler and the Judge of all nations, look mercifully on our land. Sanctify all that is rich and noble in our traditions. Grant that our ideals and aspirations may be in accordance with thy will. Take away pride and false pretense from our midst; give us humility in our relations with others and sobriety in our dealings at home. Bless our leaders and the people, in our several efforts to make this land happy and prosperous. Help us to discipline ourselves so that our national freedom may be used for the common good, and may bring us all to the knowledge of him whose service is perfect freedom, even Jesus Christ our Lord and Saviour. Amen.

THE CHURCH OF SOUTH INDIA
From *The Book of Common Worship* (1963), 56. Used by permission of Oxford University Press, New Delhi.

Communion Prayer

Almighty God and merciful Father,
we ask you
that in this communion meal,
in which we bring to mind the glorious remembrance
of the bitter death of your Son Jesus Christ,
that by your Holy Spirit,
you will work in our hearts.
May we increasingly surrender ourselves
to your Son Jesus Christ in true confidence;
so that, through the power of Your Holy Spirit,
our burdened and defeated hearts
will be fed and refreshed by his body and blood;
indeed by Him, the matchless bread of Heaven.
May we remain no longer in our sins,
but, rather, let Him live in us as we live in Him.
May we truly share in the new and eternal covenant
of your grace.
Let us not doubt that you will forever
be our gracious Father,
who no longer takes account of our sins
and who cares for all our needs—in body and soul—
as your beloved children and heirs.
Hear us, O God and merciful Father,
through Jesus Christ,
in whose name we pray along with your whole church.
Amen.

REFORMED CHURCH OF MIDDELBURG

Translated by Glenn G. Baaten from *Orden voor de Eredienst van de Gereformeerde Kerken in Nederland* (1966),
389. Used by permission of the Gereformeerde Kerken in Nederland. This prayer follows very closely
the sixteenth-century Palatinate liturgy for the Lord's Supper. An English translation of the earlier
form is used in the Christian Reformed Church and the Reformed Church in America. The prayer has
been slightly abbreviated and its language updated in the 1966 liturgy of the Reformed Church of
Middelburg in the the Netherlands. It is this 1966 prayer which has been translated from the Dutch
by Glenn G. Baaten from *Orden voor de Eredienst van de Gereformeerde Kerken in Nederland* (1966), 369.
Used by permission of the Gereformeerde Kerken in Nederland.

Prayer of Petition for the Christian Life

Grant unto us, O God,
the fullness of thy promises;
Where we have been weak,
grant us thy strength;
Where we have been confused,
grant us thy guidance;
Where we have been distraught,
grant us thy comfort;
Where we have been dead,
grant us thy life.
Apart from thee, O Lord,
we are nothing,
In and with thee, we can do all things.
Amen.

UNITED CHURCH OF CANADA
From *Service Book for the Use of the People* (1969), 299. Used by permission of the United Church of Canada.

Prayer of Confession

O Lord, with sorrow and dismay we confess before you our failure to live up to the trust committed to us. For so many years your word has been preached among us, but has yielded so little fruit. We have not given the example of redeemed lives. Because of our lack of love and joy and devotion there are still those, even among our friends and in our families, who have not yet accepted you as Savior and Lord. The power of worship of ancestral spirits is yet unbroken in our country. Even many who were once baptized and have grown up in our midst have become cold and have turned away from you, O Lord. We humble ourselves before you in shame, and plead with you, through Jesus Christ, your Son, our Lord. Amen.

THE PRESBYTERIAN CHURCH OF CAMEROON
From Presbyterian Church (U.S.A.), *Walking with Africans*, 28. Used by permission of the Presbyterian Church of Cameroon.

For the Morning
of the Lord's Day

O God, our heavenly Father, who teachest us in thy Word that there remaineth a rest for thy people, and who hast given us a promise of entering therein, grant, we pray thee, that we fail not of that promise through unbelief. May we remember the Sabbath day to keep it holy and be in the Spirit on the Lord's day.

Follow, we pray thee, the worship and teaching of thy Church this day with thy blessing. Make thy holy Word to be our nourishment, our guide, and our comfort, that by it we may be made wise unto salvation. Do thou, by all the means of grace, lead us onward in the way to heaven. Revive thy people, and turn many from the error of their ways to thyself.

Continue to bless our household, all who are dear to us, and all for whom we ought to pray, according to our individual needs. Bless all the families of the earth and cause them to know thy fatherly love. Pity and relieve the sorrows of those who mourn, and let the weary and heavy laden find rest in thee. And bring us all at last to the worship which is offered to thee on high; all which we ask in the name of our faithful Savior, Jesus Christ, to whom with thee, O Father, and the Holy Spirit, ever one God, we give all the praise, now and forever. Amen.

REFORMED CHURCH IN AMERICA
From *The Liturgy of the Reformed Church in America* (Grand Rapids: Reformed Church Press, 1968), 405–6.
    Used by permission of the publisher.

Prayer for a Meeting of the Elders

Merciful God and Father, who ruled and overruled at the council of the blessed Apostles, give us, as elders of this church, wisdom and guidance for its spiritual oversight. May our favor and influence with the people be that which comes from following Christ. Guide our deliberations, we pray thee, and direct our motives, that our thoughts, words, and actions in this meeting may be according to thy holy will. Grant that thy Church may be strengthened, and thy name glorified in the midst of thy people; through Jesus Christ our Lord. Amen.

REFORMED CHURCH IN AMERICA
From *The Liturgy of the Reformed Church in America* (Grand Rapids: Reformed Church Press, 1968), 403. Used by permission of the publisher.

For Social Misfits

In Jesus Christ, O God, you were despised and rejected by others. Watch over people who are different, who cannot copy well-worn customs, or put on popular styles of life. If they are left out because narrow people fear different ways, help us to welcome them into the wider love of Jesus Christ, brother of us all. Amen.

CUMBERLAND PRESBYTERIAN CHURCH, PRESBYTERIAN CHURCH IN THE U.S., THE UNITED PRESBYTERIAN CHURCH IN THE U.S.A.
From *The Worshipbook* (1970), 182 (adapted). Used by permission of Westminster John Knox Press.

Forgive Us Our Folly

O Lord God, we come before you in humility recognizing that we have sinned against you by governing this land with laws that oppress and cause much harm and suffering to people. We have actively followed a system based on neither love nor justice. We have resorted to violence to maintain this system, and this in turn is leading to more violence. Forgive us our folly.

We pray that you will deliver us and bring change to our situation. If it is your will to remove from office those rulers who have misgoverned and oppressed and who have misused the authority with which they have been invested, we ask for courage to do our part in this and wisdom to choose leaders who will obey your will, enact just laws and eradicate the evils and divisions that we have allowed to have dominion over us.

This we ask in the name of Jesus Christ. Amen.

THE PRESBYTERIAN CHURCH OF SOUTHERN AFRICA (1984)
From John de Gruchy, *Cry Justice: Prayers, Meditations, and Readings from South Africa* (Maryknoll, N.Y.: Orbis Books, 1986), 196. Used by permission of HarperCollins Publishers Ltd., London.

Post-Communion Prayer

Strengthen, O Lord, the hands which have been stretched out to receive thy holy things, that they may daily bring forth fruit to thy divine glory. Grant that the ears which have heard thy songs may be closed to the voice of clamour and dispute; that the eyes which have seen thy great love may also behold thy blessed hope; that the tongues which have uttered thy praise may speak the truth; that the feet which have walked in thy courts may walk in the region of light; that the souls and bodies which have fed upon thy living body may be restored to newness of life.

And with us may thy great love abide forever, that we may abundantly render back praise, praise to thine eternal majesty. Amen.

CHURCH OF SCOTLAND

From *Book of Common Order of the Church of Scotland* (1979), 26. Used by permission of Saint Andrew Press.

Communion Prayer

Holy God,
our loving Creator,
close to us as breathing
and distant as the farthest star,
we thank you
for your constant love
for all you have made.
We thank you for all
that sustains life,
for all people of faith
in every generation
who have given themselves
to your will, and
especially for Jesus Christ,
whom you have sent
from your own being
as our Savior.
We praise you for Christ's birth, life,
death, and resurrection,
and for the calling forth
of your church
for its mission in the world.
Gifted by the presence of your Holy Spirit
we offer ourselves to you
as we unite our voices
with the entire family of your faithful people everywhere.

UNITED CHURCH OF CHRIST

From *Book of Worship*, 69–70. © 1986 by United Church of Christ. Used by permission of the United Church
of Christ, Office for Church Life and Leadership.

The Recognition
of the End of a Marriage

God of all mercy,
we know that you love us even when we are not sure
that we love ourselves.
Embrace us when frustration and failure
leave us hollow and empty.
Forgive our sins,
and grant us forgiving hearts toward others.
In the confession of our lips,
show us now the promise of a new day,
the springtime of the forgiven;
through Jesus Christ,
who is able to make all things new.
Amen.

UNITED CHURCH OF CHRIST
From *Book of Worship*, 293. © 1986 by United Church of Christ. Used by permission of the United Church
   of Christ, Office for Church Life and Leadership.

Pentecost

We thank you, compassionate God,
that you sent your Spirit
to encourage those whom Jesus left behind
that they might not be alone.
Through the comfort of your presence,
you empowered them to witness to your love.

Today we also seek the encouragement of your presence.
Do not leave us alone, O God,
but send your Spirit to us
that we may worship and serve you with joy;
through Jesus our crucified and risen Savior.
Amen.

UNITED CHURCH OF CHRIST
From *Book of Worship*, 502–3. © 1986 by United Church of Christ. Used by permission of the United Church
of Christ, Office for Church Life and Leadership.

Prayer for the Ordination
of Elders and Deacons

Our merciful Father in heaven, we thank you that you have provided faithful and gifted people to serve as elders and deacons. As these new office-bearers assume their responsibilities, fill them with your Spirit, endow them with your wisdom, and grant them strength. Make them faithful workers in your vineyard. Under their guidance may your church grow in every spiritual grace, in faith which is open and unashamed, and in the committed service that promotes your reign in the world. Help them to perform their duties with enthusiasm and humility. In their work, grant them a sense of sustained awe which is rooted in daily adoration of you, their Lord. Through them may your name be honored; and your church be served.

Help us, your people, to accept them gladly, encourage them always, and respect them for the sake of your precious Son, our Lord, in whose name we pray. Amen.

CHRISTIAN REFORMED CHURCH
From *Psalter Hymnal* (1988), 1005–6. Used by permission of CRC Publications.

A Litany of Invocation

Come to us, God of peace.
Come with your healing and your reconciling power.
Come, that fear may be cast out by love;
    that weapons may be replaced by trust;
    that violence may give way to gentleness;
Come to us, God of peace.

Come to us, God of justice.
Come with your righteous judgments and your mercy.

Come, that we may hear the cries of the oppressed in every land;
   that we may see the suffering of the poor in our own land;
   that we may return to the way of righteousness and compassion;
Come to us, God of justice.

Come to us, God of love.
Come with your extravagant kindness and your goodness.
Come, that we may see you in the people of every race and culture;
   that we may embrace you in the lonely, the bereaved, and the rejected;
   that we may be an accepting and a caring church;
Come to us, God of love.

Come to us, God of unity.
Come with your forgiveness and your healing grace.
Come, that we may witness to reconciliation for a divided world;
   that we may gather around Christ's table as one people;
   that we may affirm one church, one faith, one Lord;
Come to us, God of unity.

Come to us, God of hope.
Come to us with your promises,
   come in your mysterious presence.
Come, that we may marvel at your faithfulness in past generations;
   that we may celebrate the new things you are doing among us today;
   that we may be your pilgrim people on our journey to your kingdom;
Come to us, God of hope.

UNITING CHURCH IN AUSTRALIA. Adapted from a prayer in the Opening Service of the
   Fourth Assembly of the Uniting Church in Australia (1985).
From *Uniting in Worship* (1988), 169. Copyright 1988 the National Commission on Liturgy of the Uniting
   Church in Australia.

The Renunciation of Evil Powers

The following two prayers should be used together.

Prayer of Renunciation

Heavenly Father, I confess and repent and ask You to forgive and cleanse me of all my sin. I unreservedly submit myself to the Lordship of Jesus Christ. I ask the Holy Spirit to bring to my attention all the ways in which I have been in rebellion against God. I ask You, Father, in Jesus Christ's name and through the power of His blood, to expose and bring into the light all schemes of Satan working against me (*my spouse, my children*), whether these be curses, spells, or any other evil, through any source, at any time. I ask You to bring to my attention any spiritual enemies of Jesus Christ associated with these schemes, working either within me (*my spouse, my children*) or from without. Holy Spirit, I ask You to force into the light all powers of darkness that oppress me.

In Jesus' name, and by His shed blood on Calvary, I confess and receive forgiveness for the sins of my forebears, of which I (*and my children*) are now bearing the consequences. . . .

I forsake all personal sin that has given ground to the enemy. In Jesus' name I reclaim that ground now.

I renounce all the works of the devil and commit myself unreservedly to Jesus Christ to live in obedience to His Word by the enabling of the Holy Spirit. In the Name of Jesus Christ I pray. Amen.

Prayer of Affirmation

Heavenly Father, I praise You and rejoice in Your love for me. I thank You that through Jesus Christ I have come out of darkness into God's kingdom. I praise You, Lord, that You have placed me in Christ Jesus and that You have raised me up to sit in heavenly places with Him, where all powers and authorities are now under His feet. By faith I abide in the protection and blessing of the mighty name of Jesus Christ and accept my covering by His precious blood. I pray the omnipotent power of Jesus Christ's name over myself (*my spouse, and my children named* . . .).

I joyfully confess that Jesus Christ has come in human flesh, that He died on Calvary's cross, rose again, and ascended into heaven's glory to secure my victory over sin, the flesh and the devil. . . .

I affirm that Jesus Christ's death, and my death with Him, can defeat the control and rule of sin in my life. . . .

I praise You that I am alive unto God through the power of the resurrection. In the mighty power of the resurrection that raised the Lord Jesus from the dead, I accept my enabling to walk in newness of life as God's new creation, created in Christ Jesus unto good works. . . .

Heavenly Father, I thank You that I can bring all the works of my hands to You and offer it in thanksgiving for giving me the privilege to be Your son (daughter) and to work with You. I affirm that You are owner of all that I have, and will ever have. I rejoice in my privilege to be Your steward. . . .

By faith I stand in my right to be strong in the Lord and the power of His might. . . . I choose to live as one who is more than conqueror through Jesus Christ my Lord. Thank you for saving me and infilling me with Your Holy Spirit. In the name of Jesus Christ I affirm my total dependence upon Him. In the name of Jesus Christ, I thank You. Amen.

PRESBYTERIAN CHURCH OF NIGERIA
From *The Book of Services* (1992), 251–53 (abridged).

Great Thanksgiving:
Eucharistic Prayer

Eternal God, holy and mighty,
it is truly right and our greatest joy
to give you thanks and praise,
and to worship you in every place where your glory abides.
Therefore we praise you,
joining our voices with the heavenly choirs
and with all the faithful of every time and place,
who forever sing to the glory of your name:
  (*The Sanctus: "Holy, holy, holy Lord"*)
You are holy, O God of majesty,
and blessed is Jesus Christ, your Son, our Lord.
You sent your only-begotten,
in whom your fullness dwells,
to be for us the way, the truth, and the life.
Revealing your love,
Jesus taught those who would hear him,
healed those who believed in him,
received all who sought him
and lifted the burden of their sin.
We glorify you for your great power and love at work in Christ.
By the baptism of his suffering, death, and resurrection,
you gave birth to your church,
delivered us from slavery to sin and death,
and made us a new people by water and the Spirit.
Remembering all your mighty and merciful acts,
we take this bread and this wine
from the gifts you have given us,
and celebrate with joy
the redemption won for us in Jesus Christ.
Accept this our sacrifice of praise and thanksgiving
as a living and holy offering of ourselves,
that our lives may proclaim the one crucified and risen.

(The memorial acclamation: "Christ has died, Christ is risen, Christ will come again")
Gracious God,
pour out your Holy Spirit upon us
and upon these your gifts of bread and wine,
that the bread we break
and the cup we bless
may be the communion of the body and blood of Christ.
By your Spirit unite us with the living Christ
and with all who are baptized in his name,
that we may be one in ministry in every place.
As this bread is Christ's body for us,
send us out to be the body of Christ in the world.
(Intercessions)
Help us, O God, to love as Christ loved.
Knowing our own weakness,
may we stand with all who stumble.
Sharing in his suffering,
may we remember all who suffer.
Held in his love,
may we embrace all whom the world denies.
Rejoicing in his forgiveness,
may we forgive all who sin against us.
Give us strength to serve you faithfully
until the promised day of resurrection,
when with the redeemed of all the ages
we will feast with you at your table in glory.

Through Christ, with Christ, in Christ,
in the unity of the Holy Spirit,
all glory and honor are yours, eternal God,
now and forever. Amen.

PRESBYTERIAN CHURCH (U.S.A.) AND CUMBERLAND PRESBYTERIAN CHURCH
From *The Book of Common Worship* (1993), 126–29. From *Service for the Lord's Day*, Supplemental Liturgical Resource 4, copyright © 1984 The Westminster Press. Used by permission of Westminster John Knox Press.

Maundy Thursday

O God, your love was embodied in Jesus Christ,
who washed disciples' feet on the night of his betrayal.
Wash us from the stain of sin,
so that, in hours of danger,
we may not fail,
but follow your Son through every trial,
and praise him always as Lord and Christ,
to whom be the glory now and forever.
Amen.

PRESBYTERIAN CHURCH (U.S.A.) AND CUMBERLAND PRESBYTERIAN CHURCH
From *Book of Common Worship*, 270. © 1993 Westminster/John Knox Press. Used by permission.

At the Time of an Election

Under your law we live, great God,
and by your will we govern ourselves.
Help us as good citizens
to respect neighbors whose views differ from ours,
so that without partisan anger,
we may work out issues that divide us,
and elect candidates to serve the common welfare;
through Jesus Christ the Lord. Amen

PRESBYTERIAN CHURCH (U.S.A.) AND CUMBERLAND PRESBYTERIAN CHURCH
From *Book of Common Worship*, 817. From *The Worshipbook—Services*, copyright © 1970 The Westminster
Press. Used by permission of Westminster John Knox Press.

Prayers for the Baptism of a Child

God of love, we rejoice again
to receive your grace in Word and Sacrament.
We have heard your call
and are made new by your Spirit.
Guide and guard N . . . all her days.
May your love hold her,
your truth guide her,
your joy delight her.
Bless her parents,
that she may grow up
in a secure and happy home.
Give to her family,
wisdom and courage,
laughter and peace,
and the love that endures all things.
God of grace,
in whose church there is one Lord,
one faith, one Baptism,
help us to acknowledge
that Jesus Christ is Lord,
to profess with our whole lives
the one true faith,
and to live in love and unity
with all who are baptized in his name,
through Jesus Christ our Lord,
who lives and reigns,
and is worshipped and glorified,
with you, Father, and the Holy Spirit,
one God for ever. Amen.

CHURCH OF SCOTLAND

From *Common Order* (1994), 92–93. © Panel on Worship, Church of Scotland. Used by permission.

Christmas Day

Today, O God,
the soles of your feet
have touched the earth.
Today,
the back street, the forgotten place
have been lit up with significance.
Today,
the households of earth
welcome the King of heaven.
For you have come among us,
you are one of us.
So may our songs rise to surround your throne
as our knees bend to salute your cradle.
Amen.

CHURCH OF SCOTLAND
From *Common Order* (1994), 430. © Panel on Worship, Church of Scotland. Used by permission.

Epiphany

Holy Jesus,
before your infant form
sages bowed the knee
and acknowledged your lordship
over all power and wisdom.
Grant us also clear vision and courage,
that in the light of your light,
we may devote our power and potential
to your service,
even when that requires us
to go home by another way.
Amen.

CHURCH OF SCOTLAND
From *Common Order* (1994), 431. © Panel on Worship, Church of Scotland. Used by permission.

Good Friday

Saviour of the world,
what have you done to deserve this?
And what have we done to deserve you?
Strung up between criminals,
cursed and spat upon,
you wait for death,
and look for us,
for us whose sin has crucified you.

To the mystery of undeserved suffering,
you bring the deeper mystery of unmerited love.
Forgive us for not knowing what we have done;
open our eyes to see what you are doing now,
as, through wood and nails,
you disempower our depravity
and transform us by your grace. Amen.

CHURCH OF SCOTLAND
From *Common Order* (1994), 438–39. © Panel on Worship, Church of Scotland. Used by permission.

Easter

Lord Jesus Christ, we greet you.
The cross has not defeated you,
the grave has not kept you silent.
At the first dew of the morning,
you met our sister, Mary,
and called her by her name.

We are your family and friends,
and though numbed by your death
and aware of our complicity in it,
we come hesitantly but gladly,
to confirm the rumour
that you are alive.

Meet us as you met Mary,
with gentleness and resolution.
Speak our names quietly
in our hearts,
that we may proclaim your name boldly
on our lips. Amen.

CHURCH OF SCOTLAND
From *Common Order* (1994), 440–41. © Panel on Worship, Church of Scotland. Used by permission.

For Those in the Community Services

God of all life,
you call us to live in community
and teach us to care for one another
after the pattern
of Jesus Christ your Son our Lord.
We pray for those whose position and authority
affect the lives of others.
Inspire them with a vision
of the community as it might be,
where love of neighbor
and concern for one another
drive out discontent and strife, anxiety and fear.
Help us all to work together
with one heart and will,
with sympathy and understanding,
to serve the common good,
to minister to people in trouble and despair,
and to multiply true happiness among us;
through Jesus Christ our Lord.
Amen.

CHURCH OF SCOTLAND
From *Common Order* (1994), 482. © Panel on Worship, Church of Scotland. Used by permission.

Charge and Benediction

I charge you to:
Get-to-stepping . . .
   Out into the world,
   Where God is preceeding you.

Get-to-stepping . . .
   Into the church,
   Make it the Church of Jesus Christ.

Get-to-stepping . . .
   Outside of yourselves
   And be people for others.

And now . . .
   May the Justice of God
   and the Liberation of Jesus Christ,
   And the Militant Action of the Holy Spirit,
     Be with you all,
     Now and forevermore.
Right On.

H. EUGENE FARLOUGH, JR. (1970)
Used by permission of Mrs. Arlyce J. Farlough.

Biographical Notes

(Authors still living are not dated)

Adams, Joanna

Born in Atlanta, Joanna Adams received her B.A. from Emory University and her M.Div. degree from Columbia Theological Seminary. She is the pastor of Trinity Presbyterian Church of Atlanta, Georgia, one of the largest churches in the Presbyterian Church (U.S.A.) to have a woman as pastor. She is presently the chair of the Board of Trustees for Columbia Seminary and she also chairs the Atlanta Advisory Committee for the Corporation for Supportive Housing. She is the author of numerous articles and sermons.

Alves, Rubem A.

A former minister of the United Presbyterian Church of Brazil, Rubem A. Alves is now a psychiatrist and professor in the Department of Philosophy, University of Campinas, São Paulo, Brazil. His 1969 book *A Theology of Human Hope* made him a pioneer of liberation theology in Latin America.

Andrews, James E.

Born and educated in Texas, a graduate of Austin Theological Seminary, James E. Andrews has served as a pastor, as assistant to the president of Princeton Theological Seminary, and as information officer for the World Council of Churches. He is best known as Stated Clerk of the Presbyterian Church in the United States from 1973 and then as the first Stated Clerk of the reunited Presbyterian Church (U.S.A.) from 1984 until 1996.

Baillie, Donald (1887–1954)

Preacher, theologian, and ecumenical leader, Donald Baillie taught systematic theology at St. Andrews University, Scotland. His book *God Was in Christ* was widely received as a major contribution to Christology. He was also a friend of the Student Christian Movement and the Iona Community.

Baillie, John (1886–1960)

An outstanding Scottish theologian, John Baillie served as moderator of the General Assembly of the Church of Scotland and a president of the World Council of Churches. He was also dean of divinity and principal of New College, Edinburgh. He is best known, however, for *A Diary of Private Prayer*, first published in 1936.

Barclay, William (1907–1978)

William Barclay is best known for his sixteen-volume *Daily Study Bible—New Testament* (Saint Andrew Press and Westminster John Knox Press), which has done a great deal to popularize contemporary biblical scholarship. He was born in Scotland and served as a parish minister there. He became a professor of divinity and biblical criticism at the University of Glasgow.

Barnes, Albert (1798–1870)

Albert Barnes was a pastor and author and one of the leaders in the New School branch of American Presbyterianism. Barnes was born in New York and educated at Hamilton College and Princeton Seminary. He served as pastor of the First Presbyterian Church of Philadelphia. He was accused of heresy, acquitted by his presbytery, and then ejected from the Presbyterian Church along with other New School leaders at the time of the 1837 schism. He was an ardent abolitionist and a champion of social reform.

Barth, Karl (1886–1968)

Born in Basel, Switzerland, Karl Barth did his theological studies at Bern, Berlin, and Marburg. He served as pastor in Geneva and Safenwil, Switzerland, and as professor of theology at Göttingen and Münster, then at Bonn (1930–35), where he was one of the instigators of the movement of resistance to Nazism known as the "Confessing Church." Expelled from Germany, he returned to Switzerland to teach at Basel, where his work gave rise to the movement of biblical and theological renewal that dominated the middle part of the twentieth century in Europe and much of the world. His writings include an epoch-making commentary, *The Epistle to the Romans*, and his multivolume *Church Dogmatics*, the leading monument of Reformed theology in the twentieth century. He is the major author of the Barmen Declaration, one of the confessional documents in the Presbyterian Church (U.S.A.) *Book of Confessions*.

Baxter, Patricia

Among the few women to be ordained in the Presbyterian Church of Southern Africa, Patricia Baxter has been active as an educator who is particularly concerned about the needs of women in church and society. She lectured part-time in the Department of Christianity and Society at the University of the Western Cape and the University of South Africa. She has published three books of short devotionals for women and a companion to the Bible for children.

Baxter, Richard (1615–1691)

An English Puritan, and later a Nonconformist Protestant, Richard Baxter served as a chaplain in the army of Oliver Cromwell. He was a pastor in Kidderminster from 1641 until 1660. He refused the offer of a bishopric and joined other ejected ministers as their spokesperson. His *The Reformed Pastor* is a classic interpretation of pastoral work, and his *The Saints' Everlasting Rest* is a beautiful, almost mystical description of his own spiritual life and experience. He was the chief author of the Savoy Liturgy, prepared as a common liturgy for Nonconformist churches: Presbyterian, Congregational, and Baptist.

Bayly, Lewis (d. 1631)

An English Puritan who remained within the Church of England, Lewis Bayly was the author of one of the most influential guides to the spiritual life, *The Practice of Piety*. We do not know the date of its first publication, but by 1613 it had already reached its third edition and by 1735 a fifty-ninth edition was published. New England Puritans published a translation for Native Americans in Massachusetts.

Beecher, Henry Ward (1813–1887)

The single most influential American preacher in the latter half of the nineteenth century, Henry Ward Beecher is said to have preached a mixture of civil religion and a Christianized Social Darwinism. Although he greatly modified his Calvinist roots, he never forsook them completely. His theological liberalism had great influence on both Congregational and Presbyterian ministers.

Beteta, Daniel

Born in Quetzaltenango City, Guatemala, Daniel Beteta served as a lay pastor and then as an ordained minister for fifteen years in Guatemala at the Efeso Presbyterian Church. He and his family moved to Southern California in 1989 and he became an associate pastor at Canoga Park, California, where he now serves.

Beza, Theodore (1519–1605)

A writer and theologian, Theodore Beza (de Bèze) was a friend of Calvin, and his successor in Geneva. Born in Vézelay, France, he received a liberal and humanist education. He was converted after a serious illness and went to Geneva in 1548. He taught scripture in the Academy of Lausanne, then became the first rector of the newly created Academy at Geneva, where he shared with Calvin the teaching of theology. Beginning in 1560, he became deeply involved in the life of the Reformed movement in France. Among his writings are a history of the Reformed Churches of France, a biblical tragedy about Abraham sacrificing Isaac, and a poetic version of the Psalms.

Boegner, Marc (1881–1970)

Born in Epinal, France, Marc Boegner studied law and theology at Paris. He served as pastor and as professor at the theological school of the Society of Missions. As president of the Protestant Federation of France and of the National Council of the Reformed Church of France, he was the spokesperson for French Protestantism. He was a co-president of the World Council of Churches (1948–1954). His vision of ministry was influenced first by the thought of Tommy Fallot and then by the ecumenical movement and by the theological renewal of the 1930s. His many writings include his *Cahiers* (Notebooks), published posthumously.

Bonar, Horatius (1808–1889)

Horatius Bonar was a Scottish evangelical, educated at the University of Edinburgh and ordained in 1837. He joined the Free Church of Scotland and was moderator of the Free Church General Assembly in 1883. He is best known for his hymns.

Bottoms, Lawrence (1908–1994)

The first African American to be elected moderator of the General Assembly of the Presbyterian Church in the United States, Lawrence Bottoms was born in Selma, Alabama, and was ordained by the Reformed Presbyterian Church. He joined the PCUS in 1938, served pastorates in Kentucky and Georgia, and was active on denominational boards.

Bouttier, Michel

Michel Bouttier earned a doctorate in theology and served as pastor at Saint-Laurent-d'Aigouze (a village in the south of France) and at Lyon before he became professor of New Testament at the Faculty of Theology of Montpellier. His writings that have appeared in English are: *Christianity According to Paul*, *Commentary on Ephesians*, and *Prayers for My Village*.

Bradstreet, Anne (1612–1672)

A New England Puritan whose poetry affords a remarkable glimpse into the heart and mind of Puritan New England, Anne Bradstreet was born in England and crossed the Atlantic with her husband. The mother of eight children, she spent her life as a homemaker. Most of her poems were not published until after her death.

Brousson, Claude (1647–1698)

Born at Nîmes, Claude Brousson earned the degree of Doctor of Laws and was both an attorney and a pastor in the "Desert," with the Protestant community hiding in the mountains of southern France during the persecution under Louis XIV. He began the reconstruction of the persecuted church and exhorted it to nonviolent resistance. He was executed at Montpellier.

Bucer, Martin (1491–1551)

An influential figure in shaping the Reformed tradition, Martin Bucer became a Lutheran in Heidelberg in 1518. In Strasbourg, he worked with Wolfgang Capito to lead the Reformation there. He worked hard to bring together the Reformed and Lutheran branches of the Reformation. When Calvin was exiled from Geneva and traveled to Strasbourg, Bucer received him warmly and had a great deal of influence on Calvin's liturgical development. Bucer finished his career as a professor of theology at Cambridge, having been invited to come to England by Thomas Cranmer.

Bullinger, Heinrich (1504–1575)

The German-Swiss reformer who succeeded Zwingli as pastor of the Zurich church, Heinrich Bullinger was also a theologian who wrote more than a hundred published articles on exegetical and theological topics. He was the sole author of the Second Helvetic Confession and, with Calvin, developed the Zurich Agreement on the Lord's Supper, which held together the French and German Reformed churches.

Bunyan, John (1628–1688)

John Bunyan, known as the tinker of Elstow, underwent a dramatic conversion experience and became a leading Puritan preacher, having previously served in the Parliamentary army during the English Civil War. He is best known for his monumental achievement as the author of *The Pilgrim's Progress*, which expressed a thoroughly Reformed point of view and was second to the Bible as a treasure in Reformed households from its first printing in 1678 until the middle of the twentieth century.

Calvin, John (1509–1564)

Born at Noyon, France, John Calvin studied law at Orléans and Bourges. Convinced by Lutheran ideas in 1533, he began his passage into Protestantism. After two years of moving about, he went to Basel, Switzerland, where he published the Latin edition of his *Institution of the Christian Religion* (1536). Under pressure from William Farel, he agreed to settle in Geneva to organize the Reformed church there. After a conflict with city fathers, Calvin moved to Strasbourg for three years, serving as pastor to French refugees. Recalled to Geneva in 1541, he worked there as theologian, administrator, teacher, and pastor until his death. Among his numerous works are *Institutes of the Christian Religion* (first French edition 1541), the *Geneva Catechism,* the *Treatise on the Lord's Supper*, numerous publications and commentaries on scripture, and a vast correspondence. He is the single most influential theologian for the Reformed tradition.

Campbell, Ernest T.

A native of New York, Ernest T. Campbell was educated at Bob Jones University and Princeton Theological Seminary. He served several pastorates in Pennsylvania and Michigan before being called to Riverside Church, New York. He became known as one of America's great preachers. A book of prayers, *Where Cross the Crowded Ways*, expresses his pastoral heart combined with his passion for peace and justice.

Capieu, Henri (1909–1993)

A pastor and poet, Henri Capieu served as secretary of the French Student Christian Federation in the 1930s. He was a pastor in Algiers until Algeria's independence, then he became a pastor in Paris. As the president of the Commission on Liturgy, he was the chief editor of the texts in the French Reformed hymnal, *Nos coeurs te chantent*. His poetry is both theological and Mediterranean. His final work was *De sable et de désir* (Of sand and desire).

Chalmers, Thomas (1780–1847)

A great Scottish church leader, Thomas Chalmers was minister at Kilmany and Glasgow before he became professor of divinity at Edinburgh. He was won to evangelicalism and led a group out of the Church of Scotland to organize the Free Church. He committed his life to the renewal of the church.

Corbett, Cecil

A Native American Presbyterian Church leader born in North Carolina, Cecil Corbett is Nez Percé and Choctaw. He grew up in South Dakota and was educated at Cook Christian School and Huron College. He received his ministerial education at the University of Dubuque and was the first Native American to serve as president of Cook Christian Training School (Cook College and Theological School) in Tempe, Arizona. In that capacity, he developed programs to educate Native American church leaders through the use of on-site programs. He also led Cook School to become ecumenical and international in its mission to native people from the United States, Canada, and the Pacific islands.

Costen, James

Scholar and educator of African American Presbyterians, James Costen is best known as the president of Johnson C. Smith University and dean of the Seminary. He was also president of the Interdenominational Theological Center in Atlanta, a consortium of African American seminaries of several denominations. He was elected moderator of the General Assembly of the United Presbyterian Church in the U.S.A. in 1982 and presided over that assembly again in 1983, leading it into reunion with the Presbyterian Church in the U.S.

Costen, Melva W.

Teacher, liturgical scholar, and musician, Melva W. Costen was educated at Johnson C. Smith University, the University of North Carolina, and Georgia State University. She taught music at both public school and seminary levels and has most recently served as professor of worship at the International Theological Center, Atlanta. She was the chair of the committee that produced *The Presbyterian Hymnal* in 1990.

Cromwell, Oliver (1599–1658)

A Puritan member of the Long Parliament, Oliver Cromwell served with distinction in the Parliamentary army in the English civil war waged against the crown. During the period of English history between monarchs, he served as Lord Protector. He sought to rule justly and established the precedent for Parliamentary authority in England. In the leadership vacuum brought about by his death, the crown was restored.

Csiha, Kálmán

Kálmán Csiha was born in Hungary, where he received his early schooling. When his parents were banished by the communist government in 1949, he had to finish his theological studies at Cluj in Transylvania, a region which was taken from Hungary and annexed to Romania after World War I. Arrested by the Romanian Securitate in 1957 for not volunteering a so-called criminal report on one of his colleagues, he was sentenced to ten years of incarceration in a high-security prison. After six-and-a-half years in prisons and hard-labor camps, he was released by general amnesty. He served two pastorates and organized five congregations. On May 4, 1990, after the great change in Romania, he was elected and ordained as ruling bishop of the Transylvanian Synod of Hungarian Reformed Churches. He is currently (1996) president of the consultative world synod of the Hungarian Reformed Churches.

Davies, Samuel (1723–1761)

A Presbyterian pastor and educator, Samuel Davies was born in New Castle, Delaware. He became a missionary pastor in Hanover County, Virginia, 1747–1757. In 1752 he published *Miscellaneous Poems, Chiefly on Divine Subjects*, and in 1753 he visited the British Isles with Gilbert Tennent to raise funds for the College of New Jersey (now Princeton University). He was instrumental in founding the first presbytery in Virginia in 1755. Two years later he succeeded Jonathan Edwards as president of the College of New Jersey and, like Edwards, he died in office.

de Dietrich, Suzanne (1891–1981)

Born in Niederbronn (in Alsace-Lorraine) to a family of industrialists, Suzanne de Dietrich studied engineering at Lausanne (1909–1913). She became Secretary of the French Student Christian Federation and then, in Geneva, of the World Student Christian Federation. She also worked at the Ecumenical Institute in Bossey, Switzerland. She had an itinerant ministry of wide ecumenical openness. Among her major publications were *The Witnessing Community*, *God's Unfolding Purpose*, and *Free Men*.

de Gruchy, John W.

A native South African, John W. de Gruchy is professor of religious studies at the University of Cape Town. He is also an ordained minister in the United Congregational Church of Southern Africa. His many books and articles contributed significantly to the struggle to end apartheid in South Africa.

Dickinson, Emily (1830–1886)

Although she spent her whole lifetime in Amherst, Massachusetts, and in later years rarely ventured out of her family home, Emily Dickinson has come to have great influence on generations of people through her letters and especially her poems. She was unknown and unrecognized in her lifetime but her reflections on life and faith are indications of the depth of her soul. From the window of her room, she watched the world pass by and asked questions of meaning that have had a profound influence on her readers.

Doddridge, Philip (1702–1751)

An English Nonconformist pastor and leader, Philip Doddridge served as pastor of the Independent (Congregational) chapel in Northampton and participated in an academy that prepared students for ministry. He was orthodox but a moderate in theology and was one of the first to welcome the American Awakening to England. He was excited by the work of Jonathan Edwards. His most important work was *The Rise and Progress of Religion in the Human Soul*. He is also, after Isaac Watts, the most important hymn writer of the period.

Drelincourt, Charles (1595–1669)

Charles Drelincourt served as pastor at Charenton, France, beginning in 1620 and became a renowned preacher and controversialist. Among his writings is *The Christian's Defence against the Fears of Death*.

Duck, Ruth

An ordained minister in the United Church of Christ, Ruth Duck has served churches in Wisconsin, Illinois, and Massachusetts. She is the assistant professor of worship at Garrett-Evangelical Theological Seminary, Evanston, Illinois. She has edited and contributed to several books on worship and has written several inclusive-language hymn texts. She served on the committee that produced the *Book of Worship of the United Church of Christ*.

Dwight, Timothy (1752–1817)

A congregational educator and theologian, Timothy Dwight served as a chaplain during the American Revolution. He was pastor of several churches in Connecticut, and in 1795 he became president of Yale College and professor of divinity. Under his preaching, a revival took place and a third of the students were converted by 1802. As a moderate Calvinist, he took the thought of his grandfather, Jonathan Edwards, and developed it further. He is best known for his hymn printed here.

Esquivel, Julia

A Guatemalan poet and theologian, Julia Esquivel is a member of the Presbyterian Church and has significant connections with several denominations. She graduated from the Latin American Biblical Seminary in San José, Costa Rica. Her ministry has included teaching, social service, and political activism on behalf of the poor and marginalized. Exiled from Guatemala in 1980 because of her protests against political violence, she has lived in Switzerland, Nicaragua, and Mexico, traveling widely, speaking and writing to further ecumenical cooperation in the cause of justice. A recent peace agreement has allowed her to return to Guatemala. Two volumes of her collected prayers and poems have been published in English: *Threatened with Resurrection* and *The Certainty of Spring*.

Farel, William (1489–1565)

Born in Gap, France, William Farel studied in Paris and was influenced by Jacques Lefèvre d'Etaples. This began a slow process of conversion (1518–1521). He tried evangelization in France, then went to Basel in 1523 and gathered French refugees into a congregation. After a sojourn in Strasbourg, in 1535–36 he settled in Geneva, where he successfully led the Reformation. He is best known for his power of persuasion, getting John Calvin to join him there. Opponents forced him to move to Neuchâtel (1538), where he continued his work until his death.

Farlough, H. Eugene (1938–1996)

Born in New Orleans, H. Eugene Farlough was raised in the Watts area of Los Angeles. After graduation from San Francisco Theological Seminary, he became the pastor of Faith Presbyterian Church in Oakland, California, and then became the organizing pastor of Sojourner Truth Presbyterian Church in Richmond, California. At the time of his death he was Coordinator of Student and Community Life at the Interdenominational Theological Center in Atlanta, Georgia.

Filipi, Pavel

A minister of the Evangelical Church of Czech Brethren, Pavel Filipi is professor of practical theology in the Protestant Theological Faculty of the Charles University in Prague.

Fosdick, Harry Emerson (1878–1969)

The most prominent preacher in America in the first half of the twentieth century, Harry Emerson Fosdick was a consistent champion of peace, of the new science, and of the social gospel. He wrote important interpretations of the Bible and books informed by pastoral psychology. His best-known work is *The Meaning of Prayer*. As pastor of First Presbyterian Church in New York City, he was forced out by conservative forces in 1925. Called to the Riverside Church, he served there until his retirement. During his years at Riverside, he taught preaching at Union Theological Seminary.

Glaser, Chris

A lecturer and writer, Chris Glaser is a graduate of Yale Divinity School and the author of several books, including an autobiographical work, *Uncommon Calling: A Gay Christian's Struggle to Serve the Church* (Westminster John Knox Press). From 1976 to 1978 he served on the Task Force to Study Homosexuality for the United Presbyterian Church in the U.S.A.

Graves, Geneviève

Born in Paris, Geneviève Graves was a dramatic artist and professor of dramatic art who became a Protestant in 1938. She was a member of the Protestant religious communities of Pomeyrol and Villemétrie.

Grimké, Francis (1850–1937)

Born to a slave mother and a white father, Francis Grimké escaped slavery by joining the Confederate army. He graduated from Lincoln University and Princeton Theological Seminary and was ordained as a minister in the Presbyterian Church in the U.S.A. He served as pastor of the Fifteenth Street Presbyterian Church of Washington, D.C., and was a lecturer at Hampton and Tuskegee Institutes and at Howard University. He was a champion of prohibition and of the civil rights of African Americans.

Gunning, Johann Herman (1829–1905)

Professor of theology at the City University of Amsterdam (1882–1889) and at Leiden (1889–1899), Johann Herman Gunning was also a preacher and a prolific writer. His six-volume *Life and Work* (in Dutch) includes an introduction by a successor at Leiden, K. H. Miskotte, who also wrote a book about Gunning.

Henderlite, Rachel (1905–1985)

Rachel Henderlite was the first woman to be ordained to the ministry in the Presbyterian Church in the United States and the first woman faculty member at Austin Theological Seminary. Scholar and teacher in the field of Christian education, she was a moving spirit within the Consultation on Church Union. She was also a spokesperson for the life of the mind and for justice in the world.

Henry, Matthew (1662–1714)

An English Nonconformist, Matthew Henry became a Presbyterian minister who was known as a superb biblical expositor. His *Exposition of the Old and New Testaments* appeared in several editions. Henry was a practical person whose devotional style was filled with common sense. His most important book, *A Method of Prayer*, describes his prayer practices.

Hodge, Charles (1797–1878)

America's most significant theologian of the nineteenth century, Charles Hodge taught at Princeton Seminary from 1822 until 1873 and influenced generations of students. He was a primary shaper of the Princeton theology and a leader among Old School Presbyterians. As the editor of the *Princeton Review*, he had great influence and made it one of the greatest theological journals of the time.

Hromádka, Josef L. (1889–1969)

Josef L. Hromádka was ordained as a pastor in the Evangelical Church of Czech Brethren, which he helped form as a union of Reformed and Lutheran congregations that claimed the Hussite tradition. He served as professor of theology at Jan Hus Theological Faculty in Prague from 1920 until 1939, then as a guest professor at Princeton Seminary during World War II. After the war, he returned to his country and founded the Christian Peace Conference and served as its president from 1958 until 1969. He saw communism as God's judgment on church and society. His influence and friendship with communist leaders helped to bring about the reforms of 1968.

Huber, Jane Parker

Born to Presbyterian missionary parents in China, Jane Parker Huber was raised on the campus of Hanover College, where her father was the president. She worked with Presbyterian Women's groups and served the denomination at several levels, including the committee for *The Presbyterian Hymnal* of 1990. Since 1976 she has been known as the author of many inclusive-language hymn texts set to familiar tunes.

Ibiam, Francis Akanu (1906–1995)

Sir Francis Ibiam, a Nigerian physician and statesman, was a product of the Church of Scotland Mission in Calabar, the Eastern Region of Nigeria. He became a medical missionary to his own people and founded Abiriba Hospital in 1936. He served prominently in roles of political leadership in Nigeria and Biafra. He was honored by two British knighthoods, by honorary doctorates from the Universities of St. Andrews, Scotland, Ibadan and Ife in Nigeria. His leadership in the church included service as president of the All Africa Conference of Churches and, for many years, as one of the six presidents of the World Council of Churches.

Jackson, Dora (c. 1895–1985)

A Pima, born on the Gila River Reservation at Casa Blanca, Dora Jackson was converted to Christianity and became a very active charter member of the First Presbyterian Church of Mesa, Arizona. Her prayers were collected by her friends and published after her death. The educational wing of the church building in Mesa is named after her. She was the mother of two children.

Jeszensky, Karoly (seventeenth century)

In 1674, during a period of persecution of Protestants by Jesuits and the wealthy classes in Hungary, forty-one Protestant ministers (mostly Reformed), after refusing to renounce their faith, were sold as galley slaves on ships that operated between Trieste and Naples. Karoly Jeszensky, who wrote the Hymn of the Hungarian Galley Slaves, was among those who endured this backbreaking servitude for two years. When they were released on February 11, 1676, by Dutch Admiral Michael Ruyter, the hymn was sung to celebrate their emancipation. It has become the "Ein' feste Burg" of all Hungarian Protestants. William Toth, who translated it into English in 1938 for *The Pilgrim Hymnal*, suggested the name by which the anonymous melody is now known: "Magyar" (A. C. Ronander and E. K. Porter, *Guide to the Pilgrim Hymnal*, 296).

Jones, James A. (1911–1966)

Pastor, preacher, and churchman, James A. Jones is widely remembered for his ministry at Myers Park Presbyterian Church in Charlotte, North Carolina, and as president of Union Theological Seminary in Richmond, Virginia. A selection of his eloquent prayers for the people in the context of morning worship was published as a memorial to him.

Jurieu, Pierre (1637–1713)

Pierre Jurieu, a famous Protestant apologist, was born near Blois, France. He served as pastor at Vitry-le-François and as a professor at the Academy at Sedan (1674), then as pastor of the French-speaking church of Rotterdam. He left a large correspondence by which he is remembered. His apocalyptic preaching had much to do with bringing about a renewal of a prophetic movement among Protestants in the Cévennes mountains (southern France).

Kagawa, Toyohiko (1888–1960)

A convert to Christianity at age fifteen, Toyohiko Kagawa became a world-famous Christian speaker and writer. He organized the first labor unions in Japan and evangelized the slum area of Kobe where he lived among the poor. Though he was ordained as a Presbyterian minister and served in that capacity for all of his adult life, he was an ecumenical figure.

He opposed the Japanese military and served time in jail during World War II. He was a central figure of conscience for his nation and after his death the Emperor granted him the highest designation open to a Japanese citizen.

Kapinga Esetê (d. 1975)

A committed member of the Presbyterian Church in the Democratic Republic of Congo (Kinshasa), Kapinga Esetê (Esther) was a leader among the women of her community in Mutoto and Mbujimayi. She prayed fervently in private and in women's meetings. Her missionary coworker, Mary B. Crawford, wrote down the prayer included here, translated it from Tshiluba into English, and used it widely to interpret to Americans the life and witness of the church in Zaire.

Karafiát, Jan (1846–1929)

Jan Karafiát was a minister in the Reformed Church in Prague, and after the union with the Lutherans in 1918 he refused to be a member of the united Church, called himself "reformed," and worked as a retired author and editor. He founded a journal for Reformed studies and wrote many articles. He worked on a revised version of the Bible in the Czech language.

Kerr, Hugh Thomson (1871–1950)

Born in Canada, Hugh Thomson Kerr was ordained in the Presbyterian Church U.S.A. and served pastorates in Hutchinson, Kansas, and in Chicago and Pittsburgh. He was moderator of the General Assembly in 1930 and editor of the 1946 edition of the Presbyterian *Book of Common Worship*.

Ki-Chul Joo (1897–1944)

Ki-Chul Joo was one of the most influential leaders of the Presbyterian Church in Korea during the Japanese colonial period. He was ordained in 1926 and served several churches. He became the leader of the Christian resistance movement against the imposition of emperor worship. He was arrested and tortured by the Japanese colonial police and is remembered as a martyr.

Kim, Shungnak Luke (1902–1989)

Born in Korea, Shungnak Luke Kim served as pastor of the Korean Presbyterian Church in Los Angeles from 1938 to 1959 and then moved back to Korea, becoming president of Soong Sil University in Seoul from 1959 to 1966.

Knox, John (c. 1514–1572)

John Knox was born near Haddington, Scotland. His theological studies in Glasgow turned him toward Augustine, Jerome, and the Bible. He allied himself with the Reformation in 1542. Condemned to the galleys as a slave for nineteen months, he regained his freedom in 1549 and preached intermittently in England and Scotland. He was driven into exile during the reign of Mary Tudor. During that period he lived in Geneva, among other places, and became the pastor to the English speaking congregation there. From 1559 onward, he became the great reformer of Scotland, distinguishing himself by his resistance to Mary Stuart, Queen of Scots.

Kohlbrugge, Hermann Friedrich (1803–1875)

Raised a Lutheran by parents who had left the Dutch Reformed Church because of its rationalist and modernist tendencies, Hermann Friedrich Kohlbrugge was denied ordination as a Lutheran and became pastor of an independent Reformed church in Elberfeld, Germany, from 1847 until his death. Called "the grandfather of Barmen," he took seriously the criticism of the church by Marx and Kierkegaard. He provoked a spirit of resistance within the church which, two generations later, led to the Theological Declaration of Barmen (1934). As a committed but independent Calvinist, he influenced Abraham Kuyper, Karl Barth, and Josef Hromádka.

Kölesey, Ferenc (1790-1838)

Poet, philosopher, and patriot, Ferenc Kölesey was a wealthy landowner who spurned the prerogatives of the landed gentry to take the side of the poor. A Reformed Christian, he shared in Hungary's struggle for independence from the Hapsburg dynasty of Austria, which sought to impose its Catholic faith on the Hungarian people. After Hungary finally won its independence in 1848, the prayer Kölesey had written in 1832 became, and remains, the national anthem.

Lamilami, Lazarus (1910–1977)

An ordained minister of the Uniting Church in Australia, Lazarus Lamilami held the distinction of being the first Australian Aboriginal minister in that denomination.

Lara-Braud, Jorge

Jorge Lara-Braud was born in Mexico and is a naturalized U.S. citizen. He taught theology at Austin Presbyterian Theological Seminary and at San Francisco Theological Seminary. He also served the Presbyterian Church in the United States as Director of Theology and Culture of the General Assembly Mission Board. He is presently pastor of El Buen Pastor Presbyterian Church in Austin, Texas.

Lee, Whamok Kim

Whamok Kim Lee was born in 1989, in Pyongyang, in what is now North Korea. She served as a women's evangelist in the Presbyterian Church of Korea until she came to America in 1939. She lives in Torrance, California.

Little, Sara P.

Sara Little is a recognized authority in the field of Christian education, having served as a public school teacher and professor of Christian education in two theological institutions: the Presbyterian School of Christian Education and Union Theological Seminary in Virginia, where she was the first woman on the faculty. She has served many other theological institutions as consultant, teacher, and administrator. Her writings include *The Role of the Bible in Contemporary Christian Education* and *To Set One's Heart: Belief and Teaching in the Church.*

Lutumba Tukadi-Kuetu

Lutumba Tukadi-Kuetu, a minister of the Reformed Presbyterian Church in the Democratic Republic of Congo (Kinshasa), wrote "A Prayer of the Kasai" in response to a course assignment in theology when he was a student in the Faculté de Théologie Protestante au Kasai, at Ndesha, near Kananga, Congo (Kinshasa). He chose to write this confession of his own faith as an African Christian in the form of a prayer which expresses the Reformed tradition as well as the traditional culture of the Kasai region. Hunter Farrell, the professor who made the assignment, translated the prayer from French (Tshiluba terms included) and adapted it for use in *Walking with Africans*, an educational resource for Presbyterians in the United States.

Lyte, Henry Francis (1793–1847)

Born in Kelso, Scotland, Henry Francis Lyte won three poetry prizes while a student at Trinity College, Dublin. He became a minister and served several small churches before his early death from tuberculosis. He was the author of several hymn texts.

MacDonald, George (1824–1905)

A Scottish preacher who was also a novelist, poet, scholar, teacher, and fantasist, George MacDonald has earned a high place in the ranks of those in the allegorical tradition from Bunyan to Tolkien. C. S. Lewis called him "my master." His work was not popular during his lifetime and he could barely make a living. Since his death, he has become well known as a great storyteller whose imagination captures people of all ages.

Mackay, John A. (1889–1983)

Born in Scotland, John Alexander Mackay was a Presbyterian clergyman, missionary, educator, and ecumenist. He was ordained in the Free Church of Scotland, served as an educational missionary and professor of philosophy in Peru, as Secretary for Latin America and Africa with the American Presbyterian Church's Board of Foreign Missions, as president and professor of ecumenics at Princeton Theological Seminary, and as founder and editor of the journal *Theology Today*. He was active in the founding of the World Council of Churches and served as moderator of the General Assembly of the Presbyterian Church in the U.S.A. and president of the World Presbyterian Alliance.

MacLeod, George F. (1895–1991)

Scottish pastor and founder of the Iona Community, George F. MacLeod was called from a fashionable parish in Edinburgh to Govan Old Parish Church, Glasgow. In that setting he developed his passion for justice and service to the poor. He combined radical political views with a Catholic sense of worship. He was a recipient of the Templeton International Prize for Progress in Religion and was elevated to the House of Lords. He served as president of the Fellowship of Reconciliation.

Malvezin, Caroline (1806–1889)

Caroline Malvezin was the founder of the Community of Deaconesses at Reuilly, whose creation she envisioned in a letter to Pastor Antoine Vermeil on August 31, 1841.

Manney, Ophelia

The first African American woman to be ordained to the ministry of Word and Sacrament of the Presbyterian Church west of the Mississippi, Ophelia Manney has served as a pastor and an interim pastor, and is a spiritual director.

Marguerite of Navarre (1492–1549)

Marguerite of Navarre was born in Angoulême, France, a sister of Francis I of the house of Orléans. Her religious life awakened under the influence of Jacques Lefèvre d'Etaples. Widowed, she was remarried to Henri d'Albret, king of Navarre. Without formally renouncing Catholicism, she worked for the reform of the church in all her domains. Her writings include *Mirror of the Sinful Soul* (1531) and *Spiritual Songs* (in French).

Marot, Clément (c. 1497–1544)

Born at Cahors, France, Clément Marot openly professed evangelical doctrines beginning in 1527. His thirty psalms in French metrical version were printed in 1542. After being charged with heresy and fleeing to Paris, he went to Geneva where, at Calvin's invitation, he wrote twenty more metrical psalms which were published in an enlarged edition (1543). When he died he left a large body of poetry.

Marsh, Clinton

Presbyterian pastor and African American educator, Clinton Marsh served as president of Knoxville College, Knoxville, Tennessee. He was elected moderator of the General Assembly of the Presbyterian Church in the U.S.A. in 1973.

Marshall, Catherine (1914–1984)

Catherine Marshall began a writing career as the biographer of her husband, Peter, but soon became well known as a writer and speaker in her own right. Her novels, devotional books, and prayers have sold widely.

Marshall, Peter (1902–1949)

As pastor of the New York Avenue Presbyterian Church in Washington, D.C., from 1937 until 1949, Peter Marshall became one of America's best-known preachers. He also served as chaplain of the United States Senate from 1947 to 1949. Though he died an early death, his popularity continued. Over a million copies were sold of his collected sermons, *Mr. Jones, Meet the Master*. Over two million copies of his biography, *A Man Called Peter*, written by his wife, Catherine, were sold.

Masango, Maake J.

The Presbyterian Church of Southern Africa elected Maake J. Masango to be its moderator in 1996. He directed that church's work in Christian education and in stewardship before pursuing graduate study in the United States. As pastor, educator, and advocate of peace and justice, he has helped congregations in the United States as well as in South Africa to transcend racial barriers in their life together. He is among those building a new, multiracial South Africa.

Mestrezat, Jean (1592–1657)

Famous Protestant preacher and defender of the Reformed position, Jean Mestrezat was born in Geneva and died in Paris. He served as pastor at Charenton.

Milton, John (1608–1674)

An English Puritan and a writer of political essays on behalf of the Cromwell government, John Milton is known as the poet of English Puritanism. Next to Shakespeare, he may well be the greatest poet in the English language. His three major works, *Paradise Lost, Paradise Regained,* and *Samson Agonistes* are expressions of major Reformed themes.

Mirabaud, Madame Henri (1827–1893)

Very little is known about the life of this French Reformed writer except that Madame Henri Mirabaud was the author of *Prières pour le culte de famille* (Prayers for family worship). This small volume had great influence on French Reformed devotional life for several decades.

Miskotte, Kornelis Heiko (1894–1976)

Born in Utrecht, Netherlands, K. H. Miskotte taught dogmatics and ethics at Leiden from 1945 until his retirement in 1960. Two of his works in English translation were published in the United States: *When the Gods Are Silent* and *The Roads of Prayer.*

Monod, Adolphe (1802–1856)

A pastor at Naples and at Lyon, Adolphe Monod was a professor in the Faculty of Theology of Montauban and then served as a pastor in Paris. His sermons drew large audiences.

Moody, Dwight L. (1837–1899)

Born in Northfield, Massachusetts, Dwight L. Moody became a successful businessman. In 1861, he abandoned his business and gave himself to evangelistic work. In the course of a very busy life, he organized the Sunday school movement in the United States and was a major figure in organizing the Young Men's Christian Association. He worked together with Ira Sankey from 1870 on and together they founded the Bible Institute Colportage Association in Chicago for the purpose of producing inexpensive religious literature.

Moseley, Sara Bernice

As an elder, Sara Bernice Moseley was elected president of the Women of the Church and was chair of the Board of Women's Work and the Division of International Mission of the Presbyterian Church in the United States. She was elected the first woman moderator of the PCUS General Assembly in 1978. She worked for the reunion of the Presbyterian Church U.S. and the United Presbyterian Church U.S.A. and chaired the first

General Assembly Council after reunion. In recent years, she has labored for the reunion of two congregations in her home community.

Moulin, Pierre du (1568–1658)

A famous Protestant preacher and theologian, Pierre du Moulin lived in Paris, London, Leiden, and Sedan. His writings include *Du combat chrétien* (On the Christian combat) and *Des afflictions* (On affliction).

Neff, Félix (1798–1829)

Born at Geneva and converted to the "Awakening" in a milieu influenced by the Moravians, Félix Neff became an evangelist in both Switzerland and France. He was ordained as a pastor in London. Back in France, his evangelical zeal touched off a revival.

Nelson, John Oliver (1909–1990)

An American Presbyterian minister, John Oliver Nelson spent much of his career at Yale Divinity School, where he became pastor to many students. From Yale he went on to found Kirkridge, a retreat center in the Pocono Mountains of northeastern Pennsylvania. He was a man of broad sympathies and catholic tastes, and his spirituality was part of everything he did.

Newbigin, Lesslie

Ordained by the Presbytery of Edinburgh in 1936, Lesslie Newbigin went to India as a missionary of the Church of Scotland. He was one of the founders of the Church of South India and the first Presbyterian bishop. He has served as a major leader of the International Missionary Council and the World Council of Churches. Beginning in 1974 he was a lecturer in theology in Birmingham, England, and in 1978 he was elected moderator of the United Reformed Church of England and Wales. He is well known as a speaker on the subject of world mission and is a tireless worker for the cause of Christian unity.

Ng, Greer Anne Wenh-In

Born in Hong Kong, Greer Anne Wenh-In Ng spent her childhood in Macao and was introduced to Christianity there. She is a graduate of Columbia University, New York, and is presently associate professor of Christian education at Emmanuel College, Toronto, Canada, where she is a member of the United Church of Canada.

Niebuhr, Reinhold (1892–1971)

An American German Reformed pastor, Reinhold Niebuhr went from serving as an urban pastor in Detroit to the faculty of Union Theological

Seminary in New York City. His *Moral Man and Immoral Society* shocked his fellow liberals. During World War II he abandoned his pacifism and his socialism to espouse President Franklin Roosevelt's New Deal and wartime policies.

Nuri Robins, Kikanza

Kikanza Nuri Robins has been executive of a corporation that provides training and development to both public and private sector organizations. She develops the training programs for large corporations, school districts, and not-for-profit organizations. She is a member of Brentwood Presbyterian Church, Los Angeles, and is a student at San Francisco Theological Seminary.

Oecolampadius, John (1482–1531)

Born Johann Hüssgen or Hauschein ("candlestick"), John Oecolampadius pursued humanist studies, mastered the classical languages, and combined Greek words for *house* and *lampstand* to create his Greco-Latin name. Scholar, pastor, and teacher, he was one of the pillars of the Reformation in Basel, which adopted his Reformation Act. His definition of the concept "reformed according to scripture" is particularly significant.

Paschali, Giulio Cesare (sixteenth century)

Giulio Cesare Paschali was a Sicilian gentleman and refugee at Geneva in the Italian-speaking evangelical community. From 1557 onward he was translator of Calvin's *Institutes* as well as of several books of the Bible, including the Psalms.

Patterson, Joy F.

Born in Michigan to a Congregational family, Joy F. Patterson became a Presbyterian at age twelve. A lifelong poet, she began writing hymns in 1975 and was awarded one of seven prizes offered by the Hymn Society of America in 1982. Her hymn collection, *Come, You People of the Promise*, was published in 1994 by Hope Publishing Company. She is an elder in the First Presbyterian Church of Wausau, Wisconsin, and has written more than thirty hymns.

Patterson, Thomas A. (1910–1991)

Tom Patterson was Presbyterian minister and past moderator of the General Assembly of the Presbyterian Church in Ireland. He pioneered in training church members and was the author of several books, including commentaries on the Gospels of Mark and John. He was one of the founding members of the Corrymeela Community and of other organizations working for reconciliation and peace in Northern Ireland.

Pictet, Bénédict (1655–1724)

Born and educated in Geneva, Bénédict Pictet became pastor of the parish of Saint-Gervais and later professor of theology and rector of the Academy. He became a defender of orthodox Calvinism in a time of challenge and general criticism of all religion, which was fostered by the Enlightenment. He wrote many books on ethics and on dogmatic theology and is also remembered for his hymns.

Plato, Ann (nineteenth century)

Ann Plato was a teacher in a "colored" school connected to the Fifth Congregational Church of Hartford, Connecticut. This black congregation had a history of doing its best to educate African American children. We know almost nothing about Ann Plato's life except that James Pennington, an African American abolitionist, introduced her writings to the world in order to refute the idea that blacks were unfit for anything but menial service.

Raday, Paul (1677–1733)

A diplomat and statesman, Paul Raday was a deeply religious man and the first lay leader of the Hungarian Reformed Church. As personal secretary to the leader of the Hungarian independence movement, he served as ambassador to several neighboring nations seeking to enlist their support. He published the first newspaper in Hungary. The Raday Kollegium, a faculty of the Hungarian Reformed University on Raday Street in Budapest, is named for him.

Rauschenbusch, Walter (1861–1918)

Prophet of the social gospel and one of America's most influential preachers and teachers, Walter Rauschenbusch taught at Rochester Divinity School after a career as pastor of a Baptist church in the slums of Hell's Kitchen in New York City. He incorporated his pastoral experience into his teaching and his passion for justice.

Ravasz, László (1886–1975)

Bishop László Ravasz of the Hungarian Reformed Church composed "A Prayer after Communion" in 1929 on the basis of liturgical prayers going back to the sixteenth century. Dr. Aladar Komjathy translated and published it in English in *Lift Thy Head, O Zion* (Passaic, N.J.: Hungarian Reformed Church, 1966). This prayer became part of the liturgy of the Evangelical and Reformed Church. It appears in the United Church of Christ *Book of Worship* of 1986.

Richelieu, Monsieur de (seventeenth century)

As pastor of the Reformed Church of Plouer and Saint-Malo, Monsieur de Richelieu wrote a treatise on "Saintes paraclèses pour fortifier les malades en la foi de Jésus-Christ" (Holy words of comfort to strengthen the sick in the faith of Jesus Christ), published by an elder of his church in 1659.

Rohan, Anne de (1584–1646)

Anne de Rohan was sister of the Duc de Rohan, leader of French Protestantism under Louis XIII. She was distinguished for her piety and for her general learning and culture.

Rous, Francis (1579–1659)

A Puritan leader who began as a Presbyterian and moved to a more Independent or Congregational position, Francis Rous was speaker of the House of Commons for the Long Parliament and a lay member of the Westminster Assembly. He was an ardent Calvinist with a strong mystical spirit. His book *The Mystical Marriage* expresses his passionate devotion to Christ in the form of bridal mystical imagery.

Roussel, Napoléon (1805–1878)

Pastor at Saint-Etienne, Napoléon Rousseau was deposed by the consistory (session) for his Methodist sympathies.

Rowe, Elizabeth Singer (1647–1737)

The first woman to be widely read in the English language, her earliest works were written under the pen name "Philomela." After her husband died, she retired into solitude and prayer. After her death, her friend Isaac Watts collected and published her prayers and meditations.

Schleiermacher, Friedrich D. E. (1768–1834)

German preacher, theologian, New Testament scholar and philosopher, Friedrich Daniel Ernst Schleiermacher was ordained to the ministry in the Reformed Church and participated in the formation of the union of Lutheran and Reformed churches in Prussia. He was a forerunner of several twentieth-century concerns, including an appreciation of the importance of human experience and of the social context for theology. Though remembered most widely as an academic theologian, he thought of himself primarily as a preacher—a servant of the Word. The prayers at the close of his sermons were expressions of his own experience of the living God.

Schlemmer, André (1890–1973)

Dr. André Schlemmer practiced general medicine according to the natural, nonchemical method. He was a member of the Reformed Church of France's Commissions on Liturgy and on Hymnology. His various publications include "Le Culte" (the worship service), "En Esprit et en Vérité" (in spirit and in truth), "Foi et Médecine" (faith and medicine), and "L'homme et la femme devant Dieu" (man and woman before God).

Scougal, Henry (1650–1678)

Henry Scougal was a preacher and philosophy teacher at Kings College, Aberdeen, Scotland. His best-known book was *The Life of God in the Soul of Man,* which has been republished many times and translated into several languages. George Whitefield paid it the compliment of saying that his own conversion came through reading it.

Shepherd, J. Barrie

A minister in the Presbyterian Church (U.S.A.), J. Barrie Shepherd presently serves as pastor of The First Presbyterian Church in the city of New York. He is the author of several books of prayers and poems, including *A Diary of Daily Prayer.* His latest book, *Aspects of Love: An Exploration of 1 Corinthians 13,* was published in 1995 by Upper Room Books.

Shum, James P. K.

James P. K. Shum was born in China during World War II and raised in Hong Kong. He was ordained as a minister of the Church of Christ in China and served as a pastor in Hong Kong for ten years before coming to the United States. He is presently the pastor of the Chinese Presbyterian Church of Oakland, California.

Sibbes, Richard (1577–1635)

A leading figure among English Puritan preachers and theologians of the first half of the seventeenth century, Richard Sibbes was minister of Trinity parish in Cambridge, lecturer at Gray's Inn in London, and from 1626 also Master of St. Catherine's Hall at Cambridge. His preaching gave voice to the pastoral Puritan piety of his time.

Speer, Robert E. (1867–1947)

At Princeton University, Robert E. Speer became active in the Student Volunteer Movement and in Dwight L. Moody's Northfield (Massachusetts) student conferences. He became Secretary of the Board of Foreign Missions of the Presbyterian Church in the U.S.A., serving in this capacity for forty-six years. He worked for world mission and joined John R. Mott in organizing the ecumenical mission movement, out of concern that the Christian church present a unified witness to the gospel in the world.

Spurgeon, Charles Haddon (1834–1892)

An English Baptist pastor and one of Britain's best-known preachers, Charles H. Spurgeon was pastor of New Park Street Baptist Church of London from 1854 until his death. He was a staunch Calvinist and found himself involved in theological conflicts with people on both extremes, the hyper-Calvinists on the one hand, and the non-Calvinists on the other.

Steele, Anne (1716–1778)

Born in Broughton, England, Anne Steele was the daughter of a Nonconformist pastor. For most of her life she was in ill health, which some believe may have been brought about by the death of her fiancé on their wedding day. She wrote many hymns and poems, most of them under the pen name "Theodosia." Among her works was a version of the Psalms.

Stowe, Harriet Beecher (1811–1896)

Harriet Beecher Stowe was born in Lichfield, Massachusetts, the daughter of Lyman Beecher and sister of Henry Ward Beecher. She became an ardent abolitionist and wrote *Uncle Tom's Cabin*, which appeared first in serial form in a magazine, *The National Era*. It was published in 1852 in book form and became a great success. Though she wrote several other novels, it was *Uncle Tom's Cabin* or *Life among the Lowly*, as it was first known, which made her reputation. This book was an important factor in solidifying antislavery sentiment in the North. Her collected works appeared in 1896.

Tamez, Elsa

Raised in the National Presbyterian Church of Mexico, Elsa Tamez is currently President of the Latin American Biblical Seminary in San José, Costa Rica, and a member of the Methodist Church. She is a biblical scholar who approaches theology from a Latin American perspective. Her writings and her teaching figure significantly in the struggle for peace and justice that includes an appropriate role for women in church and society.

ten Boom, Corrie (1892–1980)

Corrie ten Boom was a Dutch evangelical Christian whose convictions led her to join in the effort to hide Jews from the Nazi invaders of the Netherlands. For this "crime" she was sent to a concentration camp, where she endured terrible conditions and witnessed the death of her sister. After the war she became beloved as a speaker around the world and wrote several inspirational books including *The Hiding Place* and *Tramp for the Lord*.

Tersteegen, Gerhard (1697–1769)

Gerhard Tersteegen was a German Pietist who is best known for his many hymns, some of which have been translated into English. He expresses in them a mysticism which is thoroughly biblical. He is an excellent example of Calvinist Pietism.

Thurneysen, Eduard (1888–1974)

Born a pastor's son at Walenstadt, Switzerland, Eduard Thurneysen studied theology at the universities of Basel and Marburg. He served as YMCA Secretary at Zurich and was the pastor of several congregations, finally serving at the cathedral of Basel. His friendship with Karl Barth played a determining role in the evolution of Barth's theology.

van Dyke, Henry (1852–1933)

Both a Presbyterian minister and a literary scholar, Henry van Dyke was pastor of the Brick Presbyterian Church in New York City from 1883 until 1900. He then became professor of English literature at Princeton University, where he was a close friend of Woodrow Wilson, president of the university. He was moderator of the General Assembly of the Presbyterian Church in the U.S.A. in 1902, edited the *Book of Common Worship* of 1906, and served on the advisory committee for *The Hymnal* of 1933. He is remembered as the author of *The Story of the Other Wise Man*.

Vermigli, Peter Martyr (1500–1562)

An Italian Augustinian and scholar of scripture at Bologna, Peter Martyr Vermigli united with the Reformation and fled to Switzerland, moving to Zurich and then to Basel. He joined Martin Bucer in Strasbourg, where he lectured on the Old Testament. He went to England at the invitation of Thomas Cranmer and became Regius Professor of Divinity at Oxford University.

Viret, Pierre (1511–1571)

Pierre Viret studied in Paris, where the influence of Jacques Lefèvre d'Etaples led him to the Reformed faith. He was called in 1534 to work with William Farel and, two years later, to devote himself to the Church of Lausanne as pastor and professor for twenty-three years. A dispute over eucharistic discipline led the leaders of Berne, who controlled Lausanne, to revoke his permission to preach and teach. He continued his ministry in

France at Lyon, Nîmes, Montpellier, and in the region of Languedoc. He was called to the court of Navarre as superintendent of the churches in the region near the Spanish border south of Bordeaux.

Visser 't Hooft, Willem A. (1900–1985)

Born in the Netherlands, Willem A. Visser 't Hooft was the youngest participant in the Life and Work conference in Stockholm (1925), one of the ecumenical gatherings that led to the World Council of Churches. He had a long ministry with the YMCA and with the WSCF (World Student Christian Federation). He served as the first General Secretary of the World Council of Churches (1948–1965), and thereafter was honorary president until his death. In collaboration with Dietrich Bonhoeffer, he played a major role in the resistance to Nazism. He led the World Council toward a vision of the demands of Christian witness in the world.

Walther, Madame André (1807-1886)

A Pietist of Parisian high society, Madame André Walther inaugurated a period of Protestant feminism that lasted until World War I. She engaged in evangelization and in the first studies of the liberation of the working class in France.

Warfield, Benjamin Breckinridge (1851–1921)

A major proponent of the Princeton theology, Benjamin Breckinridge Warfield studied under Charles Hodge. He taught at Western Theological Seminary and then returned to Princeton to assume the chair of didactic and polemic theology. He had great influence through the journals he edited, *The Princeton Theological Journal* and *The Presbyterian and Reformed Review*.

Watts, Isaac (1674–1748)

Isaac Watts was educated in the Nonconformist school at Stoke Newington and became pastor of an Independent (Congregational) church in London. He became ill and was a semi-invalid most of his life. An assistant, who later became co-pastor, shared the pastoral duties. Watts wrote hymns from the age of fifteen. Thus began a revolution in Reformed worship, which previously had permitted only the singing of the Psalms. Watts's hymns "of human composure" were very popular and he became known as the father of English hymnody. Among the hymns he wrote are "Joy to the World," "When I Survey the Wondrous Cross," "Our God, Our Help in Ages Past," and "From All That Dwell Below the Skies."

Weems, Ann

Author, poet, and lecturer, Ann Weems has written many books that touch on themes of the inner life. Her workshops across the nation have been especially popular with women's groups and with people involved in the renewal of corporate worship. She lives with her husband in St. Louis, Missouri. Her writings include *Reaching for Rainbows* and *Psalms of Lament*.

Weir, Benjamin M.

Benjamin M. Weir was a missionary in Lebanon when he was taken captive by a group of extremists and held as a hostage for sixteen months. While in captivity he became nationally known in the United States. After he was freed, he was elected moderator of the General Assembly of the Presbyterian Church (U.S.A.), in 1986. He and his wife, Carol, jointly served as professors of mission and evangelism at San Francisco Theological Seminary until their retirement.

Whyte, Alexander (1836–1921)

The greatest preacher of late Victorian Scotland, Alexander Whyte was minister of St. George's Church in Edinburgh from 1870 until 1916. He was a Calvinist in theology and a Puritan in piety. He is known for his sermons, his studies of the characters of Bunyan's *The Pilgrim's Progress*, and other treatises. He was of a broad mind, welcoming the new biblical criticism and the ecumenical movement.

Wilson, Woodrow (1856–1924)

Born in a Presbyterian manse in Virginia, Woodrow Wilson became a professor at Bryn Mawr, Wesleyan, and Princeton and was elected president of Princeton University in 1902. He was elected governor of New Jersey in 1910 and President of the United States in 1912 and 1916.

Witherspoon, John (1723–1794)

John Witherspoon emigrated from Scotland to the American Colonies in 1768 to become president of the College of New Jersey. He became a leader of American Presbyterianism and served in the New Jersey legislature and the Continental Congress. He was the only minister to sign the Declaration of Independence. He convened the first General Assembly of the Presbyterian Church in the United States of America.

Wuellner, Flora Slosson

An ordained minister in the United Church of Christ, Flora Slosson Wuellner has served as an adjunct member of the faculty of the Pacific School of Religion, where her classes on prayer have been filled to overflowing. She is the author of numerous articles and books on the spiritual life, including *Prayer, Stress, and Our Inner Wounds* and *Prayer and Our Bodies.*

Wyon, Olive (1881–1966)

Born in Hampstead, London, into a cultured Victorian family, Olive Wyon was brought up in the Free Church tradition but was also devoted to Anglican sacramental practice. She was educated at St. Colm's Missionary College in Edinburgh, a Church of Scotland institution of which she served as principal for three years. She translated German theological writings, especially the works of Emil Brunner. She was active in ecumenical work, especially with the World Council of Churches, and she belonged to the Community of Grandchamp, where in 1931 a group of Reformed women began to organize themselves into a community for prayer, silence, and meditation. She wrote *The School of Prayer, The Altar Fire,* and *Prayer for Unity.*

Zwingli, Ulrich (Huldrych) (1484–1531)

The first-generation reformer who began the Swiss Reformation in Zurich, Ulrich Zwingli was an ordained priest but was strongly influenced by Christian humanism and especially by Erasmus, who led him to study the Bible. Between 1519 and 1528 he introduced reforms in Zurich, Bern, and Basel. His theological outlook was characterized as rigorously biblical, morally strict, and with a strong emphasis upon the sovereignty of God. He led the church of Zurich to eliminate all stained glass, murals, and church organs, and he banned the use of music. Because he denied that Christ was physically present in the Lord's Supper, he was unable to reach agreement with Luther at their Marburg meeting.

Bibliography

Andrews, James E. *Prayers for All Seasons*. Edited by Vic Jameson. Louisville, Ky.: Privately published, 1996.

Bachelor, Mary, ed. *The Lion's Prayers Collection*. Oxford: Lion Publishing Company, 1992.

Baillie, John. *A Diary of Private Prayer*. New York: Charles Scribner's Sons, 1949.

Baird, Charles W. *The Presbyterian Liturgies*. Grand Rapids: Baker Book House, 1957.

Barclay, William. *A Barclay Prayer Book*. Oxford: SCM Press; Valley Forge, Pa.: Trinity Press International, 1990.

Barnes, Albert. *Prayers for the Use of Families*. Philadelphia: Charles De Silver & Sons, 1850.

Barth, Karl. *Selected Prayers*. Translated by Keith R. Crim. Richmond: John Knox Press, 1965.

Bayly, Lewis. *The Practice of Piety*. London: Printed for Daniel Midwinter, and the Three Crowns in St. Paul's Church-yard, 1714. Reprint, Morgan, Pa.: Soli Deo Gloria Publications, 1995.

Bouttier, Michel. *Prayers for My Village*. Translated by Lamar Williamson. Nashville: Upper Room Books, 1994.

Bullinger, Heinrich. *Small Christian Prayerbook*. Zurich: Rudolff Wolffen, 1623.

Bunyan, John. *Divine Emblems*. Vol. 4 of *The Entire Works of John Bunyan*. Edited by Henry Stebbing. Toronto: Virtue, Yorston & Co, n.d.

Calvin, John. *Opera quae supersunt omnia*. Vol 6. In *Corpus Reformatorum*. Braunschweig: C. A. Schwetschke & filium, 1863–1900.

Carden, John. *With All God's People: The New Ecumenical Prayer Cycle*. Geneva: WCC Publications, 1989.

Chapal, Roger, and Jean Pellegrin, eds. *La tradition calvinienne* (The Calvinist tradition). Prières de tous les temps, no. 27. Chambray, France: Editions C.L.D. (Cahiers du Livre et du Disque), 1981.

Christian Reformed Church. *Psalter Hymnal.* Grand Rapids: CRC Publications, 1934.

Christian Reformed Church. *Psalter Hymnal* (1988). Grand Rapids: CRC Publications, 1988.

Church of Scotland. *A New Directory for the Public Worship of God.* Edinburgh: Macniven and Wallace, 1898.

Church of Scotland. Committee on Public Worship and Aids to Devotion. *The Book of Common Order.* Edinburgh: Saint Andrew Press, 1979.

Church of Scotland, *Book of Common Order of the Church of Scotland.* Edinburgh: Saint Andrew Press, 1994.

Church of South India. *The Book of Common Worship.* Madras: Oxford University Press, 1963.

Csiha, Kálmán. *Light through the Bars.* Translated by David P. Szekeres. Revised by Bernard Woudenberg. Poems translated by Stephen Szabo. Richmond Heights, Ohio: "The Light" Publication Project, n.d. [1996].

Cumberland Presbyterian Church, United Presbyterian Church in the U.S.A., and Presbyterian Church in the U.S. *The Worshipbook.* Philadelphia: Westminster Press, 1970.

Davies, Horton. *The Communion of Saints: Prayers of the Famous.* Grand Rapids: Wm. B. Eerdmans Publishing Co., 1990.

de Gruchy, John W. *Cry Justice: Prayers, Meditations and Readings from South Africa.* Maryknoll, N.Y.: Orbis Books, 1986.

Dickinson, Emily. *Selected Poems and Letters of Emily Dickinson.* Edited by Robert N. Linscott. Garden City, N.Y.: Doubleday & Company, 1959.

Doddridge, Philip. *The Rise and Progress of Religion in the Soul.* Philadelphia: Presbyterian Board of Education, n.d.

Duck, Ruth C. *Flames of the Spirit: Resources for Worship.* New York: Pilgrim Press, 1985.

Esquivel, Julia. *Threatened with Resurrection.* Elgin, Ill.: Brethren Press, 1982.

Evangelical Alliance. *The History, Essays, Orations and Other Addresses of the Sixth General Conference of the Evangelical Alliance.* New York: Harper, 1875.

Evangelical Church of Czech Brethren. *Agenda Českobratrské církve evangelické* (Liturgical handbook). Prague, Czech Republic: Evangelical Church of Czech Brethren, 1988.

Evangelical Church of Czech Brethren. *Evangelický Zpěvník (Hymnbook).* Prague, Czech Republic: Evangelical Church of Czech Brethren, 1979.

Evangelical Church of Czech Brethren. *Sbírka kázání* (Sermon collection). Prague, Czech Republic: Evangelical Church of Czech Brethren, 1993.

Ferguson, James, ed. *Prayers for Public Worship.* New York: Harper & Brothers, 1958.

Fosdick, Harry Emerson. *The Meaning of Prayer*. New York: Follett Publishing Co., 1949.

Fox, Selina Fitzherbert. *A Chain of Prayer across the Ages*. New York: E. P. Dutton & Co., 1943.

Glaser, Chris. *Coming Out to God: Prayers for Lesbians and Gay Men, Their Families and Friends*. Louisville, Ky.: Westminster John Knox Press, 1991.

God's Minute. Philadelphia: VIR Publishers, 1916.

Grimké, Francis J. *The Works of Francis J. Grimké*. 4 vols. Edited by Carter G. Woodson. Washington, D.C.: Associated Publishers, 1942.

Gunning, J. H. *Gebed voor het huisgezin* (Prayers for the household). 2d ed. Utrecht: G.H.A. Ruys, 1908.

Hambrick-Stowe, Charles. *Early New England Meditative Poetry: Anne Bradstreet and Edward Taylor*. Mahwah, N.J.: Paulist Press, 1988.

Hromádka, Josef L. *Sbírka kázání* (Sermon collection). Prague, Czech Republic: Evangelical Church of Czech Brethren, 1952.

Huber, Jane Parker. *A Singing Faith*. Philadelphia: Westminster Press, 1987.

Jones, James A. *Prayers for the People*. Richmond: Union Theological Seminary and John Knox Press, 1967.

Kagawa, Toyohiko. *Songs from the Slums*. Nashville: Abingdon-Cokesbury Press, 1930.

Ki-Chul Joo. *I Will Offer My Blood* (in Korean). Seoul, Korea: Hyesung Publishing Co., 1968.

Kieling, Jered, ed. *The Gift of Prayer: A Treasury of Personal Prayer from the World's Spiritual Traditions*. New York: Continuum, 1995.

Knox, John. *The Works of John Knox*, edited by David Laing. 6 vols. Edinburgh: James Thin, 1895.

Kohlbrugge, Hermann Friedrich. *Gebeden uitgesproken bij de openbare godsdienstoefeningen* (Prayers offered in public worship). Amsterdam: Vereeniging tot Uitgave van Gereformeerde Geschriften, 1950.

Lewis, C. S., ed. *George MacDonald: An Anthology*. New York: Macmillan Co., 1947.

MacLeod, George F. *The Whole Earth Shall Cry Glory: Iona Prayers by Rev. George F. MacLeod*. Glasgow: Wild Goose Publications, 1985.

Marshall, Catherine. *Adventures in Prayer*. New York: Ballantine Books, 1975.

Marshall, Peter. *Mr. Jones, Meet the Master*. New York: Fleming H. Revell Co., 1949.

Miskotte, K. H. *Gevulde Stilte: enkele Gebeden en Preken* (Pregnant silence: selected prayers and sermons). Kampen, Netherlands: J. H. Kok, 1974.

Presbyterian Church in the U.S. *New Psalms and Hymns*. Richmond: Presbyterian Committee of Publication, 1901.

Presbyterian Church in the U.S., Cumberland Presbyterian Church, United Presbyterian Church in the U.S.A.: Joint Committee on Worship. *The Worshipbook*. Philadelphia: Westminster Press, 1990.

Presbyterian Church in the U.S.A. *The Book of Common Worship*. Philadelphia: Presbyterian Board of Publication and Sabbath School Work, 1906.

Presbyterian Church in the U.S.A. *The Book of Common Worship*. Philadelphia: Presbyterian Board of Christian Education, 1932.

Presbyterian Church in the U.S.A. *The Book of Common Worship*. Philadelphia: Presbyterian Board of Christian Education, 1946.

Presbyterian Church in the U.S.A. *The Hymnal*. Philadelphia: Presbyterian Board of Christian Education, 1933.

Presbyterian Church (U.S.A.). *The Book of Common Worship*. Louisville, Ky.: Westminster John Knox Press, 1993.

Presbyterian Church (U.S.A.). *The Presbyterian Hymnal*. Louisville, Ky.: Westminster John Knox Press, 1990.

Presbyterian Church (U.S.A.). *Gifts from Latin Americans: A Celebration of Life*. Louisville, Ky.: Mission Interpretation and Promotion, Congregational Ministries Division, Presbyterian Church (U.S.A.), [1996].

Presbyterian Church (U.S.A.). *Walking with Africans: Beginning the Journey*. Louisville, Ky.: Mission Interpretation and Promotion, Congregational Ministries Division, Presbyterian Church (U.S.A.), [1995].

Presbyterian Outlook, The (Richmond), vol. 152 (1970), nos. 8 (Feb. 23) and 15 (Apr. 13).

Reformed Church in America. *The Liturgy of the Reformed Church in America, together with the Psalter*. Edited by Gerrit T. Vander Lugt. New York: The Board of Education, 1968.

Reformed Church of Middelburg. *Orden voor de Eredienst van de Gereformeerde Kerken in Nederland*. Kampen, Netherlands: J. H. Kok, 1966.

Ronander, Albert C., and Ethel K. Porter. *Guide to the Pilgrim Hymnal*. Philadelphia/Boston: United Church Press, 1966.

Rous, Francis. *The Mystical Marriage* or *Experimental Discoveries of the Heavenly Marriage between a Soul and her Saviour*. London: Printed by R. W. for John Wright, at the Kings-head, 1656.

Rowe, Elizabeth Singer. *Devout Exercises of the Heart*. Edited by Isaac Watts. Baltimore: J. Kingston, 1811. Original publication, 1737.

Scougal, Henry, *The Life of God in the Soul of Man*. Philadelphia: Westminster Press, 1948.

Shepherd, J. Barrie. *Diary of Daily Prayer*. Minneapolis: Augsburg Publishing House, 1975.

Speer, Robert E. *Five Minutes a Day*. Philadelphia: Westminster Press, 1943.

Spurgeon, Charles. *Prayers from a Metropolitan Pulpit*. New York: Fleming H. Revell, 1906.

Spurgeon, Charles. *Sermons of Reverend C. H. Spurgeon of London*, 19 vols. New York: Funk & Wagnalls Co., 1887–1888.

Stebbing, Henry, ed. *The Complete Works of John Bunyan*, 4 vols. New York: Johnson Reprint Corp., 1970.

Suter, John Wallace. *Prayers for a New World*. New York: Charles Scribner's Sons, 1964.

Taizé Community. *Praise God: Common Prayer at Taizé*. London: Oxford University Press, 1977.

ten Boom, Corrie. *This Day is the Lord's*. Old Tappan, N.J.: Fleming H. Revell Co., 1979.

Thorne, Leo S., ed. *Prayers from Riverside*. New York: Pilgrim Press, 1983.

United Church of Canada. *Service Book, People's Edition*. Toronto: United Church Press, 1969.

United Church of Christ. *Book of Worship*. New York: United Church of Christ, Office of Life and Leadership, 1986.

United Church of Christ. *The Pilgrim Hymnal*. Boston: Pilgrim Press, 1958.

Uniting Church in Australia. *Uniting in Worship: People's Book*. Melbourne: Uniting Church Press, 1988.

Vermigli, Peter Martyr. *Sacred Prayers Drawn from the Psalms of David*. Vol. 34 of *Sixteenth Century Essays and Studies*. Edited by John P. Donnelly and Joseph McLelland. Kirksville, Mo.: Thomas Jefferson University Press and Sixteenth Century Journal Publications, 1996.

Washington, James Melvin. *Conversations with God: Two Centuries of Prayers by African Americans*. New York: HarperCollins, 1994.

Weeks, Louis B., "John Witherspoon, Presbyterian Revolutionary," *Presbyterian Survey* 65 (September 1975): 5–7.

Weems, Ann. *Psalms of Lament*. Louisville, Ky.: Westminster John Knox Press, 1995.

Weir, Ben and Carol. *Hostage Bound, Hostage Free*. Philadelphia: Westminster Press, 1987.

Whyte, Alexander. *Family Worship*. Glasgow: Blackie & Son, 1891.

World Student Christian Federation. *Venite Adoremus II: Prayers and Services for Students*. Geneva: World Student Christian Federation, n.d.

Wuellner, Flora Slosson. *Prayer, Fear, and Our Powers*. Nashville: Upper Room Books, 1989.

Wyon, Olive. *The Altar Fire*. London: SCM Press, 1954.

Zwingli, Ulrich. *Early Writings*. Edited by Samuel Macauley Jackson. Durham, N.C.: The Labyrinth Press, reprinted 1987.